The Di

Tom Brinkmann

Brian Buniak

Steve Carper

Carolyn Cosgriff

Clark Dissmeyer

Peter Enfantino

Vince Nowell, Sr.

James Reasoner

Ward Smith

Robert Snashall

Bob Vojtko

Joe Wehrle, Jr.

Edited by Richard Krauss

The Digest Enthusiast (TDE) Book Ten
Published twice a year by Larque Press LLC

Editor/Designer: Richard Krauss
Cover: The Creature from the Black Lagoon, as seen in the classic, Universal Pictures trilogy, by Richard Krauss.
Cartoons: Bob Vojtko (page 19)

Printed on demand from June 2019 in the United States of America and other countries.

Larque Press LLC
4130 SE 162nd Court
Vancouver, WA 98683

Visit <larquepress.com> for news about current digest magazines and vintage digest covers. Join our mailing list for exclusive updates on *The Digest Enthusiast* and other Larque Press projects.
Sign up at <larquepress.com>

Back cover images:
Mike Shayne Mystery Magazine Vol. 45 No. 7 July 1981
Mechanix Illustrated May 1954
Charlie Chan Mystery Magazine Vol. 1 No. 3 May 1974
Harlem Model Bronze Books No. 1 1952
Startling Mystery Stories No. 2 Fall 1966
Manhunt Detective Story Monthly Vol. 2 No. 6 August 1954

Our thanks to our contributors for some of the cover images that appear in this edition. Cover images are retouched to remove defects from the original source material. When reference material is not available, retouched areas are “best guess.” In some cases text may be reset in a font similar to the original work.

The Digest Enthusiast
ISSN 2637-448X (print)
ISSN 2637-4498 (Kindle)
ISBN 978-1072025610

Interview

Articles

Synopses

Reviews

Fiction/Poem

Departments

On newsstands, with *Mike Shayne Mystery Magazine* Vo. 41 No. 2 (page 25), in Aug. and Sept. 1977.

News Digest

Black Cat Mystery Magazine No. 4 brought news **Carla Coupe** would leave her post as co-editor with **John Betancourt** in May, after the 2019 Malice Domestic mystery convention—replacement TBA. During the event held in Bethesda, Maryland plans were finalized, and **Michael Bracken** is taking over the reins. And there's more news from Michael, "My story "Oystermen" is scheduled for the July/August issue of *Ellery Queen's Mystery Magazine* and, while attending Malice Domestic, I recorded the story for *EQMM*'s podcast. "Sex Toys" will appear in *Knucklehead Noir* (Coffin Hop Press); "Gracie Saves the World," co-authored with **Sandra Murphy**, will appear in *The Book of Extraordinary Historical Mystery Stories* (Mango); and "Love, or Something Like It" will appear in *Crime Travel* (Wildside Press).

"I am the co-creator and co-editor (with **Trey R. Barker**) of *Guns + Tacos*, a novella anthology series from Down & Out Books that begins releasing monthly episodes in July. I wrote the second novella in the series, "Three Brisket Tacos and a Sig Sauer," and the bonus story offered only to subscribers, "Palatanos Con Lechera and a Snub-Nosed .38." I'm also editor of *The Eyes of Texas*, an anthology about Texas private eyes, featuring stories from 17 writers with ties to Texas, which Down & Out Books will release this fall." <downandoutbooks.com>

Associate editor of *Alfred Hitchcock* and *Ellery Queen*, **Jackie Sherbow** sent the following: "The July/August issue of *AHMM* contains the annual Black Orchid Novella Award winner. In Sep/Oct, you'll find a Mystery Classic by **G.K. Chesterton**, introduced by **Marvin Lach-**

man. Nov/Dec will contain the next installment in **Leslie Budewitz's** award-winning Stagecoach Mary series. This year, stories from *Alfred Hitchcock's Mystery Magazine* tied to win the Agatha Award for Best Short Story at the Malice Domestic conference; they were "All God's Sparrows" by **Leslie Budewitz** and "The Case of the Vanishing Professor" by **Tara Laskowski**, both from the May/June 2018 issue. In the spring, **Janice Law** was nominated for a Derringer Award for her story "The Crucial Game" from the Jan/Feb 2018 issue, and at the Edgar Awards banquet, editor **Linda Landrigan** was presented with the Ellery Queen Award from the Mystery Writers of America. Currently, **Emily Devenport's** story "10,432 Serial Killers (In Hell)" from the May/June 2018 issue is nominated for an International Thriller Award. Please note that submissions to the next Black Orchid Novella Award contest, in coordination with The Wolfe Pack, are open until May 15, 2020.

"The July/Aug issue of *Ellery Queen's Mystery Magazine* contains a Black Mask Department story by **Tara Laskowski**, winner of this year's Agatha Award for Best Short Story, as well as tales by Edgar winners **S.J. Rozan** and **Peter Turnbull**, multiple International Thriller Award winner **Twist Phelan**, and SMFS Lifetime Achievement Award winner **Michael Bracken**. The Sep/Oct issue features a nonfiction article by Edgar winner **Joseph Goodrich** about **Manfred B. Lee's** recently unearthed correspondence, and stories by MWA Grand Master **Bill Pronzini** and Hammett Prize and Grand Prix de Littérature Policière recipient **James Sallis**. The

Nov/Dec issue will contain new stories by **Doug Allyn**—multiple *EQMM* Readers Award winner—and *New York Times* bestseller **Charlaine Harris**, among others—as well as the annual Readers Award ballot. In April, **Art Taylor** was presented with the Edgar Allan Poe Award for Best Short Story for his "English 398: Fiction Workshop" from the July/Aug 2018 issue of *EQMM*. This year, stories from the magazine were also nominated for the Arthur Ellis and Agatha Awards. Currently, "Window to the Soul" by **Scott Loring Sanders** (from the Sep/Oct 2018 issue) is nominated for an International Thriller Award and "English 398: Fiction Workshop" by **Art Taylor** as well as "Bug Appétit" by **Barb Goffman** (Nov/Dec 2018) are nominated for the Anthony Award, to be presented at Bouchercon 2019 in Dallas."

The editor of *Pulp Modern*, **Alec Cizak**, and I have finished the Summer 2019 issue, released in

May. See the ad on page 137 for a list of its authors. To capture a more classic pulp look-and-feel, Alec switched the photo-based images we've used in recent editions to illustrations. Our thanks to **Rick McCollum** (cover), **Brian Buniak** (back cover), **Alfred Klosterman**, **Ran Scott**, and **Dan W. Taylor** for their interior illustrations—and **Bob Vojtko** for four new cartoons. Alec also has a collection of macabre stories, *Lake County Incidents*, coming this Summer from ABC Group Documentation. Don't miss it.

Justin Marriott sent in this update: "One recent publication and three forthcoming titles to announce from The Paperback Fanatic house of fanzines which are devoted to vintage paperbacks. All are full-colour throughout, heavily illustrated and available through Amazon. In case you had missed it, *The Paperback Fanatic* 41 was a 64-page Conan special with articles on the famous barbarian in paperbacks and comics, novels based on the BBC's eco-horror cult TV series Doomwatch, the boundary-pushing "plantation pulps" inspired by the success of *Mandingo*, novelizations of classic Australian films, a profile of top Doctor Who writer **Brian Hayles** and an interview with paperback cover artist **Raymond Kursar**.

"The third issue of *Hot Lead* will be published by 1 June, a 52-page special devoted to the 'adult western', the enduringly popular genre that mixed sex and six-guns. It includes a definitive study of the history of the adult western, a visual guide to western themes in sleaze paperbacks, overviews of key series such as The Trailsman, Ruff Justice, Lassiter and Cimarron. Plus a bonus top 10 of western comics.

"The twelfth issue of *Men of Violence* will be a double issue containing over 100 reviews of men's adventure paperbacks featuring iconic characters such as The Executioner, The Destroyer, The Butcher and The Death Merchant, as well as rare and outrageous titles from lesser known publishers. Published on 1 July, this will be black and white with a lower cover price to reflect this.

"Then the debut issue of *The Monster Maniac* will follow later in the summer. Devoted to horror magazines and comics, the first issue is scheduled to contain an interview with **Stephen 'Taboo' Bissette**, articles on **Tom Sutton**, underground horror comics and pre-code rarities."

Variety reports upcoming shows on Apple's new streaming service will include new episodes of **Steven Spielberg's** *Amazing Stories*. ". . . Spielberg said that 'Amazing Stories' will explore 'a universal human trait to search for meaning.' The director also teased that one episode of the series will dive into the story of a World War II pilot who transports through time." Publisher **Steve Davidson** said the fourth issue of *Amazing Stories* magazine is being readied for a Summer 2019 release. In addition to an all-new story by **David Gerrold**, it features **Gary Dalkin, Jack Clemons, M.J. Moores, Jen Frankel, Tatiana Ivanova, Cathy Smith, Brad Preslar, Brian Rappatta, Joanna Miles, Shirley Meier, Ricky Brown**, and **Steve Fahnestalk**.

Josh Pachter wrote to say, "My fiftieth-anniversary story "50" placed second in the 2018 *EQMM* Readers Award balloting, and "If It's Tuesday, This Must Be Murder" was a finalist for the 2018 Best Short Story Derringer. The May/June *EQMM* includes "A Study in Scarlett!," which is the first in a series of five stories bringing back Ellery Queen and

the Puzzle Club; the second and third stories ("The Adventure of the Red Circles" and "The Adventure of the Black-and-Blue Carbuncle") have already been purchased.

"Coming up in *EQMM* are a nonseries story ("The Secret Lagoon," set in Iceland) and a translation for the "Passport to Crime" department (Dutch author **Anne van Doorn's** "The Poet Who Locked Himself In"), and I also have a story called "The Yellow Rose of Texas" in **Michael Bracken's** forthcoming *The Eyes of Texas* anthology. Meanwhile, **Dale Andrews** and I are finishing up work on *The Further Misadventures of Ellery Queen*, which should be out from Wildside Press by the end of the year."

Rick Ollerman was beset by a series of maladies recently, which forced delays on his projects. Nonetheless he says, "the next issue of *Down & Out: The Magazine* is being revived from its unplanned hiatus. This will feature a new story by **Walter Satterthwait**, as well as stories by the award-winning

Brendan DuBois, **Benjamin Boulden**, **Sylvia Warsh**, a collaboration by **Ray Daniel** and **Kellye Garrett**, **Robb T. White**, and more. Our featured column by **J. Kingston Pierce** is a wonderful piece on one of **Erle Stanley Gardner's** "other" series, the D.A. Doug Selby novels. The new issue should be finished in a couple of weeks.

"I'm also editing the anthology for the 50th anniversary Bouchercon, *Denim, Diamonds and Death*, anthology which will be published by Down & Out Books and released at the conference in October."

Congratulations are in order for **Art Taylor** who reports: "I won this year's Edgar Award for Best Short Story for "English 398: Fiction Workshop" from *EQMM*'s July/August 2018 issue. I also have a new story, "Better Days," in the current (May/June 2019) issue of *EQMM*. That's it for digest magazines—though I do have a story, "Hard Return," scheduled for the *Crime Travel* anthology in early December."

John Linwood Grant, editor of *ODQ*, sent in this update: "Having got *Occult Detective Quarterly* No. 5 out in February, the *ODQ* team is currently finalising two more issues of *ODQ* for this year, with a wide range of strange tales coming up. Plans include the return of **Brandon Barrows'** Japanese spirit investigator, **Sam L Edwards'** hard-bitten Joe Bartred, and **Melanie Atherton Allen's** period character Simon Wake—plus a host of exciting new acquisitions from both experienced and emerging writers. Reviews, retrospectives and art will add to the blend, taking readers across the range of the whole occult detective sub-genre. *ODQ* No. 6 is expected Summer 2019, and *ODQ* No. 7 for Autumn/Fall."

Science fiction and fantasy author **Edd Vick** reports, "*Cirsova* ('The Magazine of Thrilling Adventure and Daring Suspense') will publish a Summer Special issue in

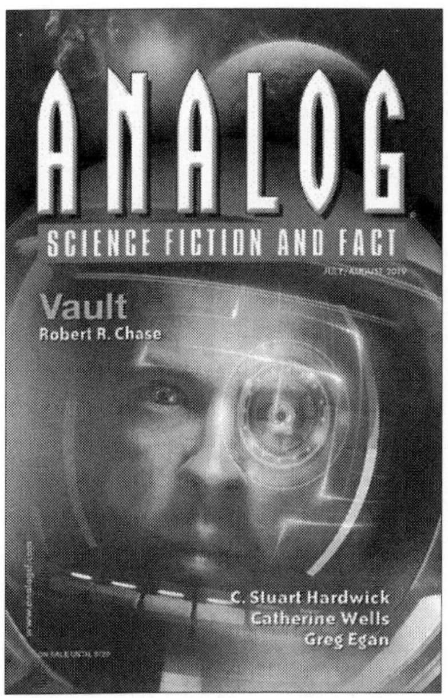

2019 to feature longer stories. One of those stories will be "The Ghost of Torreon", by me and **Manny Frishberg**, a pulp adventure tale set in 1914, featuring a man who develops the astounding ability to travel over radio waves. Beto uses his newfound skill in aid of Pancho Villa and the Mexican Revolution. This story will also be included in my first short story collection, *Truer Love and Other Lies*, coming in November from Fairwood Press <fairwoodpress.com>.

Associate Editor of *Analog* and *Asimov's*, **Emily Hockaday** sent in the following: "The biggest news coming from *Analog* is that Jan/Feb 2020 is our official ninetieth anniversary issue. We have an exciting anniversary event that is free and open to the public: *Analog Science Fiction and Fact* and New York City College of Technology are partnering to celebrate 90 years of *Analog*! All are invited to 'An Astounding 90 Years of *Analog Science Fiction and Fact*: The Fourth Annual City Tech Science Fiction Symposium' on Thursday, December 12th, for a daylong event featuring academic papers, readings, and panel discussions. Follow *Analog* on Facebook and Twitter or visit City Tech's website for more information and to RSVP: <openlab.citytech.cuny.edu/sciencefictionatcitytech/annual-symposium>. In addition to the symposium, *Analog* will also be celebrating its 90th anniversary throughout all of 2020 with a special throwback cover design, as well as retrospectives of classic stories. We'll have stories from *Analog* regulars, newcomers, and superstars throughout the year.

"We also have great things to come for the rest of 2019: Stories from **Greg Egan**, **Catherine Wells**, **Martin L. Shoemaker**, **Alison Wilgus**, **Norman Spinrad**, **Julie Novakova**, **Guy Stewart**, **Aimee Ogden**,

Jay O'Connell, and more! **Adam-Troy Castro** revisits Minnie & Earl with our cover story for Sep/Oct; fans of his Nebula-nominated story "Sunday Night Yams at Minnie and Earl's" and newcomers alike won't want to miss this exciting novella. We'll be giving the Sep/Oct issue away at the Brooklyn Book Festival, along with our sister publications, Sunday September 22nd from 10 a.m.–6 p.m. Come visit our booth at Brooklyn Borough Hall for give-aways, a special subscription rate, and to meet authors and editors.

"*Asimov's Science Fiction Magazine* has a lot of great fiction in store: Our July/Aug cover story is **Suzanne Palmer's** thrilling and satisfying "Waterlines." In the same issue, **Ian McHugh** gives us a "Story with Two Names" on an ecologically intricate planet at odds with human colonization. This issue also features **Dominica Phetteplace**, **Ray Nayler**, **Maggie Shen King**, and more. *Asimov's Science Fiction's* annual slightly spooky Sep/Oct issue is filled with chills and thrills! Stories by **D. Mercurio Rivera**, **Andy Duncan**, **Stephanie Feldman**, **Sandra McDonald**, **Gord Sellar**, **James Sallis**, **Megan Arkenberg**, **Michael Libling**, **Rich Larson**, **Kristine Kathryn Rusch**, and others will set your spine tingling! A new *Asimov's* anthology, edited by Sheila Williams and published by Prime Books, goes on sale in early September 2019, titled *Asimov's Science Fiction Magazine: A Decade of Hugo & Nebula Award Winning Stories, 2005–2015*.

"We'll be giving the Sep/Oct issue away at the Brooklyn Book Festival, along with our sister publications, Sunday September 22nd from 10 a.m. – 6 p.m. Come visit our booth at Brooklyn Borough Hall for giveaways, a special subscription rate, and to meet authors and editors. **Andy Duncan** will be visiting the booth to sign books and magazines!"

Doug Draa, editor of *Weirdbook* wrapped up his second annual in Feb. 2019, themed: Cthulhu. Regular issues have fallen a bit behind schedule, but he's optimistic *Weirdbook* No. 41 will be out in June 2019. Issue No. 42 will be a special issue made up entirely of stories by **John Shirley**. Subsequent issues have filled up quickly, so Doug won't be able to accept new submissions until late in 2020. Stay tuned for news on future *Weirdbook Annuals.*

Lesann Berry is working on a collection of supernatural short stories. "Short pieces I've been compiling for a couple of years. It covers a wide range of genres including speculative, spooky entities, more traditional ghost stories, some more supernatural creepy stuff, etc. In general, things that go bump in the night all wind up in this collection." *Uncanny Echoes* is scheduled for release this fall/winter.

Harry Warren, from England, wrote to share a letter he received from **Ed Emshwiller** (sent on Feb. 10, 1963), in response to his inquiry about painting technique. Here's what Ed wrote (spelling corrected):

> *In painting a S.F. cover I generally make pencil roughs after reading the story. When I have a couple which seem to express dramatically some aspect of the story I transfer the drawings to illustration board. The roughs are the size of the finished reproduction. I do the roughs on tracing paper so I can trace on the back side the main outlines and then burnish with a table knife the drawing onto the illustration board. The illo board has a 1/2 or 1 inch border masked off by masking tape. Then using casein paints or Winsor Newton designers colors I paint the small roughs well enough to give the impression of the finished work. These sketches are submitted to the editor, art director, or publisher (depending on the routine of the publication). A selection of one sketch or the other, with any suggestions for changes, is made at that time.*
>
> *With a sketch O.K.'d, I return to the tracing paper and make a new drawing twice the finished size of the reproduction. In some cases larger still, up to 3 1/2 or 4 times, although up 2 times is most usual and most publications prefer it. After getting the drawing 'right' I transfer it in the same manner I did with the roughs. Often in finishes I paint a little extra around all four sides and matte it with regular matte board to the size I think it should be. The reason for the extra painting is so that the art director can juggle the size and position if necessary to get type in place. However I prefer to do as on the small roughs; that is to mask off a border of a couple of inches which I remove when finished painting leaving the white illustration board around the painting. That system is the one I use whenever I know there will be no need to juggle.*
>
> *As to the actual painting I generally put down an underpainting of the basic colors for different parts of the painting. Then I modify and work detail into the various parts after the entire underpainting is done. I work in casein and designers colors principally because*

they dry rapidly. In working with them I use a variety of brushes and palette knives.

The outline I've given above is the usual procedure I follow. However I enjoy working in various media and I have used inks, crayons, oils, watercolors, dyes etc. along with airbrush, stippling, splatter, floating colors, etc. Some publishers who particularly like my work don't require sketches in color, just a pencil rough or two, and in some cases don't ask for sketches at all, just finished paintings.

In general I suggest you might do a series of paintings illustrating favorite stories. I don't know your work but feel most young artists need a lot of figure drawing and painting practice. That coupled with doing finishes as 'professionally' competent as possible is a good program. To get started as an illustrator usually requires a portfolio of good work and the best way to get one is turn out at least a couple dozen finishes as well as you can, select the best half a dozen, and submit them preferably in person, to the publishers.

Good luck.

–Ed EMSHwiller

Our thanks to Harry, and to **Susan Emshwiller** for their permission to share EMSH's letter with *TDE*'s readers.

As always, **Scotch Rutherford** has been busy: "First off, we're going to be releasing our 2019 Special Issue, "Switchblade: Tech Noir" in early fall. *Switchblade* Issue Ten, will be out in early July, with a cover featuring *Switchblade Stiletto Heeled* editor, **Lisa Douglass**. I am

a contributing author to the new Down & Out anthology, "Greaspaint & 45s." with my story "Payasos Asesinos. I also have a story in *Broadswords & Blasters* Issue 9, titled "Termination Clause" [See our *B&B* No. 9 review on page 134.]

Editor **J.D. Graves** sent in this blurb for *EconoClash Review* No. 4: "The elemental number: Earth-wind-fire-books . . . I mean air. Four is the tetrad . . . the perfect number . . . a number for all mankind. These stories pulse with realism as they swing wildly between genres and bring you the joy in other people's pain. The one, the only **Rex Weiner** kicks things off with a fantastic peek into realistic crime and punishment; and the one, the only, **A.B. Patterson** closes the show with the most transgressive thing I've read outside a public lavatory. Everyone in between brings

vivid, pulse pumping action and suspense mixed nicely with severe moments of WTH. *ECR* No. 4 proudly features the authors: **Mark Slade**, **Jon Zelazny**, **Robert Petyo**, **Hailey Piper**, **Matthew X. Gomez**, **Mark Slade**, **J.L. Boekenstein**, **Hatebreaker**, **J.S. Rogers**, and **C.W. Blackwell**. Buy this book—lock the door with a chair—and get down with the fourth issue of *EconoClash Review*.

"*ECR* is still trying to be the only biannual pulp rag that prints more than a two issues a year. For a special edition I am considering something along the lines of War Noir. It could include all aspects of the world between the Vietnam war years, including hippies, covert CIA LSD trials, CReEP, Apocalypse Now fan fic, Nixon vs Lizard People, paranoid PKD style realism). Still feeling out the vibe from other authors."

Phyllis Galde, Editor-in-Chief of *Fate* magazine says issue No. 734 will be out on newsstands in June. Its theme is haunted castles. Other themes for issues to come include tattoos, and how different cultures employ them. "The world is so crazy now and so much violence is rampart. Want to address that too."

Check out your local Barnes & Nobel. It's one of the best outlets for digest magazines, including *Nostalgia Digest*. The summer edition should be out by the time you read these words. Here's what's in store per editor **Steve Darnall**: "The Summer 2019 issue of *Nostalgia Digest* includes a cover story about the remarkable career of **Agnes Moorehead**, along with articles about **Mae West**; the early career of **Burt Lancaster**; **Teddy the Wonder Dog**, one of Hollywood's first canine heroes; **Bing**, **Frank** and the first generation of "crooners;" the golden age of humor fiction; memories of Chicago baseball in the 1940s and '50s . . . and of course, the complete schedule for our weekly radio show *Those Were the Days*—now in its 50th year on the air!"

Mystery writer **Robert Lopresti** has stories in the queue with *Alfred Hitchcock* and *Black Cat Mystery Magazine*. One of his yarns for Hitchcock features his series character "Shanks."

It's always great to receive letters of comment on *TDE*. **Tore Stokka** wrote from Norway, "May I suggest you do an interview with **John Gregory Betancourt**? He's got stories in *AHMM*. Besides, he's publishing three digests thru his Wildside Press.

"I was hoping someone would do an article on the digests **RAP** was involved with—and here it is—and everything I hoped it would be. Thanks. (A few of the digests got rather short shrifts, but maybe someone else will give them an in-depth look later on.)" Tore also suggested articles on *Spaceway*, *Venture SF*, and *Jack London*. "Maybe someone could do a 'think piece' on 'What is in a name (digest-wise)?'" Great ideas Tore, thanks for sending them!

Co-editors **Matthew X. Gomez** and **Cameron Mount** sent in this update about their digest magazine: "*Broadswords and Blasters* will be publishing issues 10 and 11 this year in July and October. As always, it strives for the "professional weird" vibe, with stories featuring time-travelling gnomes, mecha romance, apocalypses on Sundays, Polynesian warriors, post-apocalyptic landscapes, mystic assassins, and living holy books. While *Broadswords and Blasters* absolutely publishes sword-and-sorcery (broadswords) and retro-scifi (blasters), it remains dedicated to publishing high quality action stories regardless of subgenre. *Broadswords and Blasters* will reopen for submissions in October 2019."

Managing Editor of *Pulp Literature,* **Jennifer Landels**, wrote this

about issue No. 23, coming for Summer: "Have a sip of summer wine with **Kelly Robson**, enter mythic worlds with **Lena Zaghmouri** and **Christian Walter**, crack the code of another Fairmount Manor Mystery by **Mel Anastasiou**, peek into sixteenth-century Ecuador with an excerpt of *What the Wind Brings* by **Matthew Hughes**, and read the final chapters of Allaigna's Song: Aria by **JM Landels**. All this plus poetry by **Casey Reiland**, **Raluca Balasa**, **Alison Braid**, and **Lola Street** with **Chaille Stovall**, as well as flash fiction from **Susan Pieters**, **Deborah Davitt**, **Josephine Greenland**, and **Zoë Johnson**."

Publisher **Chuck Carter** sent in the lineup for *Mystery Weekly Magazine* July 2019: **Jay O'Connell**, **Robert C. Madison**, **Don McLellan**, **Bill Connor**, **Shannon Hollinger**, **Chris Wheatley**, and **Stacy Woodson**. Chuck and **Kerry Carter's** new cover artist is **Robin Grenville-Evans**, who created the covers for both the June and July issues.

Richard Kellogg wrote, "Airship 27 has just released my new children's book, *Barry Baskerville and the Buried Treasure*. Available at the Amazon website, the mystery is Volume Six in a series of stories about boy detective Barry Baskerville. The book is beautifully illustrated in color by noted Hawaiian artist, **Gary Kato**. In this story, Barry must use all his skills of observation and deduction to decipher a code and locate a hidden treasure. Young readers will be exposed to the legend of Sherlock Holmes while improving their problem-solving abilities at the same time."

Look for *Paperback Parade* No. 104 in the June–July timeframe. Editor/Publisher **Gary Lovisi** says, "The issue will have a long extensive article by me and **Art Scott** on the US Signet Carter Brown paperbacks, focusing on the **McGinnis** covers, among other things, not yet set."

The third issue of **Nigel Taylor's**

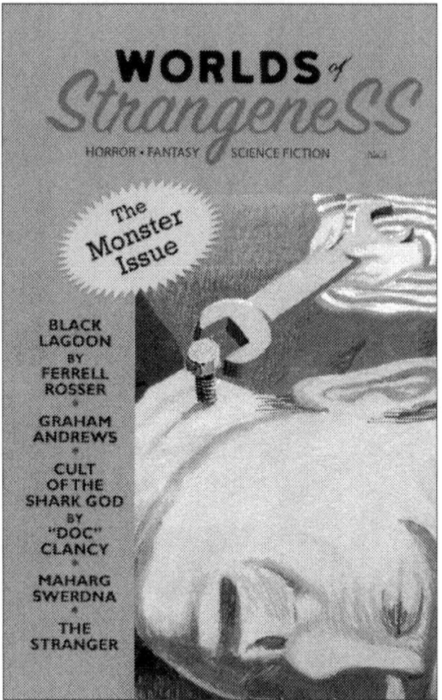

WORLDS of
Strangeness
HORROR • FANTASY • SCIENCE FICTION
The Monster Issue
BLACK LAGOON BY FERRELL ROSSER
GRAHAM ANDREWS
CULT OF THE SHARK GOD BY "DOC" CLANCY
MAHARG SWERDNA
THE STRANGER

Worlds of Strangeness debuted in May 2019. This issue is printed on demand and distributed by Amazon, which will help increase awareness and sales of this independent horror, fantasy, and science fiction digest. (See my review of No. 2 [Oct. 2017] on larquepress.com or Goodreads.)

Lifelong Californian, **Vince Nowell**, who wrote the piece on RAP mentioned earlier, also sent an LOC of his own. "First, the cover. *Great!!* To get an Emsh front cover—even if published previously—is a great achievement. Congratulations. The Interview with **Susan Emshwiller** was a top-notch feature. Very interesting, very well done, and very unique." We have Susan to thank on all counts. Her interview was the feature most often mentioned in the feedback I've heard. Another chapter in *TDE*'s mission to record bits of digest history.

To finish off this issue's "News Digest" with gusto, **Gordon Van**

Acknowledgments My thanks to *TDE*'s readers and contributors for your support. Many of the enthusiasts who helped spread the word about *TDE9* are listed below. All comments and ratings are greatly appreciated. My apologies if I've left anyone out.

Advertising
American Bystander <americanbystander.org>
EconoClash Review <econoclash.com>
Pulp Literature <pulpliterature.com>
Pulp Modern <pulp-modern.blogspot.com>
Switchblade <switchblademag.com>

Blog Posts/Newsletters
Michael Bracken <crimefictionwriter.com>
AHMM <facebook.com/alfredhitchcockmm>
Pulp Literature <pulpliterature.com>
Josh Pachter <facebook.com/josh.pachter>
EQMM <facebook.com/elleryqueenmm>
<jamesreasoner.blogspot.com>
<SandraSeamans.blogspot.com>
Rudolf Schütz <rubberaxezine.com>
Bill Thom <PulpComingAttractions.com>
Kevin Tipple <shortmystery.blogspot.com>

Booksellers
Bud's Art Books, Mike Chomko Books, Dreamhaven Books and Comics, and Modern Age Books

Ratings/Reviews/Listings
(Amazon, Goodreads) John Adkins, Steve Alcorn, Lee Bay, Lesann Berry, Willy Boy, Alec Cizak, Robert Garbarino, Tim Goebel, Tony Goins, J.D. Graves, Cecilia Dunbar Hernandez, J.M. Hunter, Karl, Karla, Kim, Gazmend Kryeziu, Jennie, Joe, Joseph, Laj, Mike Lazur, Mary, Ron Morreale, Moudry, Michael Neno, Osiris Oliphant, Kipp Poe, Rachel, Kate Sherrod, Stacy, Steven, and Scott Walker.

Social Media Posts, Shares, and Likes
(Pinterest, Twitter, Facebook, etc.)
Graham Andrews, Ann Aptaker, Bill Baber, Rusty Barnes, JM Beck, Leslie Berry, David Brinkmann, Micki Browning, Mary Burgess, Gary Bush, Cindy Callaghan, James Cassara, C.F. Carter, Bobbi Chukran, Alec Cizak, Bruce Coffin, Adrian Cole, Steve Cooper, Carla Kaessinger Coupe, Chris DeVito, Paul Di Filippo, Deborah Elliott-Upton, Peter Enfantino, Tracy Falenwolfe, Robert Fasnacht, Grant P. Ferguson, Eve Fisher, Kathleenellen T. Ford, Tim Fuller, Eric Gahagan, John Gaynard, Laurie Gienapp, Barb Goffman, Lorie Lewis Ham, Vera Holubec-Brad Haas, Bruce Harris, Dawn Frank Hearn, Jim Hendrickson, Julie Herman, Aimee Hix, Reiner Frank Hornig, Adam House, David Hyman, Clemmie Jackson, Dean James, Eleanor Cawood Jones, Ann Kellett, Mohamed Osman Khalifah, Carol Kilgore, Jessica Knutzen, Rachel Krauss, JM Landels, Robert Lopresti, Alice Loweecey, Andrew MacRae, Jeffery Marks, Paul D. Marks, Justin Marriott, Paula J. Matter, Janis Susan May, Rick McCollum, Rosemary McCracken, James McCrone, Sandra Murphy, Velma 'Negotiable,' O'Neil De Noux, Kathleen Banks Nutter, Laura Oles, John O'Neill, Alan S. Orloff, Josh Pachter, Dennis Palumbo, Charlotte Phillips, William Dylan Powell, Richard Prosch, Jean Maurie Puhlman, Lori-Ann Reif, Risa Rispoli, Michael Samerdyke, Mary Bakos Sebesta, Kipp Poe Speicher, JJ Stick, Alice Quay Stovall, Mary Lederman Sutton, Art Taylor, Gloria Teague, Mark Thielman, Kevin Tipple, Dave Truesdale, Albert Tucher, Karen Turner, Bob Vojtko, Temple Walker, Cynthia Ward, James Lincoln Warren, and Stacy Bolla Woodson.

Gelder, publisher of *The Magazine of Fantasy and Science Fiction*, tells us the July/Aug issue will include stories by **G. V. Anderson**, **Albert Cowdrey**, **Alex Irvine**, and **Cassandra Khaw**. "And our 70th anniversary issue (the Sep/Oct 2019 issue) is going to be a good one. We've got a cover by **David A. Hardy**. The lineup for the issue isn't final yet, but we will probably have new stories by **Paolo Bacigalupi**, **Elizabeth Bear**, **Kelly Link**, **Ken Liu**, **Maureen F. McHugh**, and **Michael Moorcock**. We'll also have the last story **Gardner Dozois** wrote." Gordon caps things off with the preview (above) of the July/Aug cover by Mondolithic Studios.

Bob Vojtko's Cartoon Digest

"What amazes me is how such weird looking things can make a space ship."

"What could have caused these books on the top shelf to suddenly fall?"

"If this is your first trip to Earth, press 1."

James Reasoner

Interviewed by Richard Krauss

A professional writer for more than forty years, James Reasoner has authored several hundred novels and short stories, garnering praise from *Publishers Weekly*, *Booklist*, and the *Los Angeles Times*. His books appeared on the *New York Times* and *USA Today* bestseller lists. He lives in Texas with his wife, award-winning fellow author Livia J. Washburn.

Photo by Livia J. Washburn

The Digest Enthusiast: From your blog <jamesreasoner.blogspot.com>, it's easy to tell you're a voracious reader as well as a million-words-a-year writer. When did the fiction bug first strike, and how have your tastes changed over the years?

James Reasoner: My mother liked to read, and there were always a few books around my parents' house when I was a kid. My first "favorite" was a Little Golden Book called *Scuppers the Sailor Dog* by Margaret Wise Brown, illustrated by Garth Williams. I know that now because I looked it up and actually bought a copy a few years ago to read it again decades later. It actually holds up pretty well and is a cute, well-written, well-illustrated story. I also remember my mother reading a Little Golden Book featuring Lassie to me. Clearly, I was a fan of dog books.

What really set me off as a reader, though, happened when I was six years old. The little town in Texas where I grew up didn't have a public library until a few years later (that's another story), but every Saturday, the bookmobile came out from the big library in the county seat and parked under a tree on Main Street. My sister, who was a teenager at the time, checked out books from it, and one Saturday she took me with her. From the moment I set foot in that big, panel truck of a bookmobile and saw more books than I'd ever seen in one place before, I was hooked. Man, was I hooked. The kids' books were on the bottom shelves, naturally, and over the next few years I worked my way through just about all of them, checking out as many as I was allowed to, reading them during the week, and going back the next Saturday for the next armful. A couple that I particularly remember were the juvenile novelizations of the Disney movies *Twenty Thousand Leagues Under the Sea, Davy Crockett, King of the Wild Frontier* and *Davy Crockett and the River Pirates*. I loved those and read them over and over. That binge lasted for about five years, which would have made me eleven or so by the time the bookmobile stopped coming out. By that time, I had graduated to the adult mysteries, Westerns, and science fiction books. I recall checking out Mike Shayne books (*This is It, Michael Shayne*); Perry Mason novels by Erle Stanley Gardner and Donald Lam/Bertha Book novels by his pseudonym A.A. Fair; Hopalong Cassidy books by Clarence E. Mulford, Powder Valley books by "Peter Field" (a house-name, but back then I didn't even know such a thing existed), and Westerns by Zane Grey and Max Brand. I think I checked out *Dune* from the bookmobile, but I wouldn't swear to it. I know I got Isaac Asimov's Lucky Starr, Space Ranger books there.

So how have my reading tastes changed since then? Ummm . . . well . . . they've expanded, I guess you could say. But the sort of stuff I loved reading back then . . . I still love reading it as much as ever. (What am I on now, my fourth or fifth childhood? I lose track.)

TDE: When did you first try your hand at writing a story yourself and how did it progress to the first publication of your work?

JR: The first time I put a story on paper I was ten years old and in the fifth grade. But before that, I was making up stories. Toy guns were very popular among me and my friends as we grew up in the late Fifties and early Sixties, but when we played, rather than just running around and pretending to shoot each other, I insisted on coming up with characters we could pretend to be and reasons why we were running around pretending to shoot each other. My friends probably thought I was crazy, but they put up with me. I realize now those were the first stories I ever "wrote."

But the first one I actually wrote down . . . that came about because one of the local TV stations ran the *Sons of Hercules* series, which was a syndicated package of thirteen Italian "sword and sandal" movies. I watched those over and over and loved them, so I finally decided to write my own sword and sandal epic. I don't remember the title or anything else about it except the hero's name was Argustus. I've never written anything else remotely like that, as far as I recall. My second story, written shortly after that, was much more indicative of the way my career would go: it was a cowboys vs. rustlers shoot-em-up called "Gunsmoke in the Valley." The more things change, etc., etc.

I continued writing stories for my own entertainment and that of any friends I could badger into reading them. Within a year or so I was writing mystery novels (each actually 30–40 pages of notebook paper covered front and back with my cramped scrawl, so probably more like 12–15,000 word novellas) very much influenced by the Hardy Boys, but starring me and a group of my friends (and my dog) as the detectives. I did probably a dozen of these, and by the time I finished, the last one actually was novel-length. At that point I was well into my "secret agent" phase, and the stories had turned into action/adventure yarns. I also wrote a Tarzan novel that had a strong espionage/secret agent element to it and probably 30,000 words of a Lone Ranger novel that I never finished. All these stories are long since gone.

By the time I was in college I had figured out that I wanted to be a professional writer and was buying issues of *Writer's Digest*. I wrote dozens of mystery, science fiction, horror, and fantasy stories and sent them out to every market that I could dig up. None of them ever sold or got anything except a printed rejection slip, except for one mystery story that was sent back from *Mike Shayne Mystery Magazine* with a personal note from Cylvia Kleinman Margulies, the editor at the time. And I think she was just being nice to an eager kid. I was still several years away from selling anything to *MSMM* or any other magazine. I never tried to write a novel and sell it in those days. That just seemed too daunting. So I concentrated on short stories, had no luck, and had just about given up on ever being a writer when I got married and my wife Livia encouraged me to try again. That's when I finally started selling.

TDE: There were a number of semiprozines being published in the 1970s and 1980s. Gordon Linzner's *Space & Time*, *Hardboiled*, and another title, *Skullduggery* that changed its name to *Spiderweb* in 1982. All of them published your work. What do you recall about those days, working with those editors?

JR: The only other small press magazine I sold to, as far as I recall,

Space & Time No. 67 Winter 1985/86
with Reasoner's "Bugeyes"
Cover by Ron Wilber

Skullduggery No. 5 Winter 1981
with Reasoner's "Dreams Before Breakfast"
Cover by Frank Hamilton

was *Just Pulp*. I don't remember anything about it except that I came across a listing for it somewhere and sent them a post-apocalyptic science fiction story I'd done called "Season of Storms". The story had made the rounds of the professional SF magazines without selling, but *Just Pulp* took it. I don't remember if it was a paying market or just contributor's copies, but if there was any money involved, it wasn't much. Looking at the listing for the magazine in the Fictionmags Index, I see that the editor was Thomas R. Rankin (didn't remember that) and that it lasted for seven issues (I was in the third one). The only other author I recognize among the contributors is John D. Nesbitt, who's now a well-known and highly regarded Western writer.

Space & Time was another case of finding a listing for a magazine that might be a home for one of my science fiction stories that had failed to sell at any of the pro markets. Gordon Linzner was the editor and his name was familiar to me. I wasn't deep into SF fandom then, but I know now that *Space & Time* had been around for a while, was around for a lot longer after I sold that story to them, and has a good reputation as a small press magazine. The story I did was called "Bugeyes" and was about encounters between Terran miners and one of the natives on a colony world.

Hardboiled was edited and published by Wayne Dundee, and Wayne and I had mutual friends. I'm sure it was one of them who pointed me in the direction of the magazine. We quickly became good friends and remain so to this day. *Skullduggery/Spiderweb* was edited at one

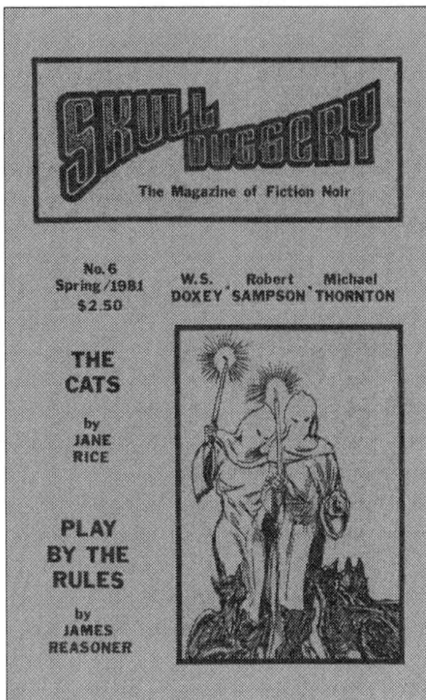

Skullduggery No. 6 Spring 1981
with Reasoner's "Play By the Rules"
Cover by Doreen Greeley

Skullduggery No. 7 Summer 1981
with Reasoner's "The Double Edge"
Cover by Frank Hamilton

point by Will Murray, who I knew through pulp fandom, and I know he bought at least one of the stories I sold there. All the issues of both those magazines were nicely done, and I enjoyed writing for them, even though there was little or no money involved. I believed in the stories and was glad I could get them out there for people to read. I guess they were the Seventies and Eighties equivalents of today's webzines. The community of writers that grew up around them was a close-knit one, and there are probably at least a dozen authors published in those magazines who are still my friends.

TDE: Glad you didn't give up on *Mike Shayne Mystery Magazine*, as things turned out they published a lot of your stories in the late 1970s and early 1980s, beginning with "Comingor" in August 1977. Was that your first big sale?

JR: Yes, it was. After the little hiatus where I'd stopped submitting for a while, I had started sending stories to *MSMM* again, and by this time Sam Merwin Jr., who was actually the magazine's first editor back in 1956, had returned to edit it again. Sam never sent me a printed rejection slip. He sent me hand-written rejections scrawled on whatever piece of scratch paper was handy, and he always told me why he was rejecting a story and encouraged me to send more. I learned a lot from those notes and owe Sam a real debt of gratitude for taking the time to write them. I sent him a sort-of police procedural story called "Haven", and he wrote back to say that if I'd make a couple of changes in it, he would buy it. Of course, I was happy to make those changes, but while I was doing that he bought "Comingor" without

Spiderweb No. 3 Summer 1982
with Reasoner's "Dead In Friday"
Cover by Frank Hamilton

Mike Shayne Mystery Magazine August 1977
with Reasoner's "Comingor"

any revisions. And then he took the revised version of "Haven", so it became my second sale. And speaking of "Comingor", more than forty years later I'm thinking seriously about writing a new story set there, for an anthology to which I'll be contributing later this year.

Comingor, for those interested, is the name of a small, fictional Texas town based very loosely on Comanche, Texas, the county seat of Comanche County where a lot of my relatives lived at one time or another.

TDE: Good to know. You wrote several series with PIs for digests: Markham, Cody, and Delaney. I'm not sure any of their first names were ever mentioned in their adventures. What else can you tell us about them?

JR: No, none of those guys have first names! Well, I guess they do, but I don't know them. Cody came first, but in novel length, not short stories. I wrote the first Delaney story very soon after writing *Texas Wind*, Cody's debut. The novel was in first-person and very much influenced by Ross Macdonald's Lew Archer books, while "Three Birds" (*MSMM*, January 1979), the first Delaney story, was in third-person and a deliberate attempt to write a more realistic, private eye procedural. The second one, "The $100,000 Collar" (*MSMM*, March 1979), was more of the same. "All the Way Home" (*MSMM*, April 1979), the first Markham story, was a switch back to first person and my take on the classic Southern California private eye. I was writing these while I was trying to sell *Texas Wind*, so a lot of my time in those days was taken up with private eyes.

I think there was another Delaney story, but I'm darned if

MSMM Jan. 1979 with Reasoner's "Three Birds" Cover by Sid Bingham

MSMM March 1979 with Reasoner's "The $100,000 Collar"

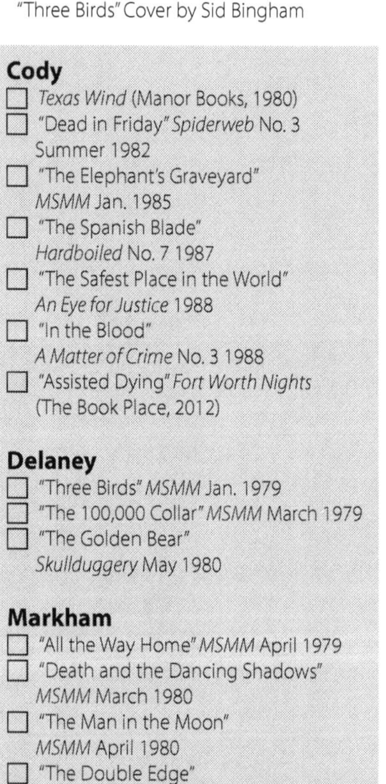

Cody

- ☐ *Texas Wind* (Manor Books, 1980)
- ☐ "Dead in Friday" *Spiderweb* No. 3 Summer 1982
- ☐ "The Elephant's Graveyard" *MSMM* Jan. 1985
- ☐ "The Spanish Blade" *Hardboiled* No. 7 1987
- ☐ "The Safest Place in the World" *An Eye for Justice* 1988
- ☐ "In the Blood" *A Matter of Crime* No. 3 1988
- ☐ "Assisted Dying" *Fort Worth Nights* (The Book Place, 2012)

Delaney

- ☐ "Three Birds" *MSMM* Jan. 1979
- ☐ "The 100,000 Collar" *MSMM* March 1979
- ☐ "The Golden Bear" *Skullduggery* May 1980

Markham

- ☐ "All the Way Home" *MSMM* April 1979
- ☐ "Death and the Dancing Shadows" *MSMM* March 1980
- ☐ "The Man in the Moon" *MSMM* April 1980
- ☐ "The Double Edge" *Skullduggery* Summer 1981
- ☐ "War Games" *MSMM* April 1982

I can figure out what it was. "The Golden Bear," maybe, from the May 1980 issue of *Skullduggery*. After all this time, too many of these stories are just titles to me.

The other Markham stories are "Death and the Dancing Shadows" (*MSMM*, March 1980), "The Man in the Moon" (*MSMM*, April 1980 [see page 89]), "The Double Edge" (*Skullduggery*, Summer 1981), and "War Games" (*MSMM*, April 1982 [see page 91]). So, five stories total, and I don't think there will ever be any more.

I wrote more stories about Cody than any other private eye (except for Mike Shayne, of course): "Dead In Friday" (*Spiderweb*, Summer 1982), "The Elephant's Graveyard" (*MSMM*, January 1985), "The Spanish Blade" (*Hardboiled* No. 7, 1987), "The Safest Place in the World" (*An Eye for Justice*, 1988), and "In the Blood" (*A Matter of Crime* No. 3, 1988). Those last two appeared in original anthologies, not maga-

MSMM April 1979 with Reasoner's "All the Way Home"

MSMM March 1980 with Reasoner's "Death and the Dancing Shadows"
Cover by Bill Edwards

zines. I would have said that there would never be any more Cody stories after that, but when I gathered up the older ones to be reprinted in a book called *Fort Worth Nights*, I decided to write a new one to go with them, and the result was "Assisted Dying", a novella that appears only in that book. It's unlikely that Cody will return, but you never know. If a good idea occurs to me, I wouldn't mind doing another one.

TDE: All three have pages over at <thrillingdetective.wordpress.com>. You wrote over two dozen Mike Shayne short novels for the magazine under the Brett Halliday house name. How did you move from selling your own short stories to ghosting these novelets?

JR: As I mentioned above, I always got along well with Sam Merwin Jr., the editor of *MSMM*, and in one of our pieces of correspondence about some short story I'd sold him, I asked a question about a recent Mike Shayne story in the magazine. I don't recall what I asked, but when Sam wrote back to me, he asked if I'd like to try my hand at one of the Shaynes. He said they ran 20,000 words and paid "a flat, lousy 300 bucks". Well, at that point in my career, $300 didn't sound lousy to me at all. I told Sam I'd be thrilled to write a Shayne story (he knew I was a long-time fan of the character). He sent me the Mike Shayne bible, which he had written at some point, maybe all the way back in the Fifties during his first stint as editor on *MSMM*. It had a lot of background information on Mike Shayne, his supporting cast, the Miami setting, etc. Most of it was stuff that I knew from reading the Shayne novels, but it was good to have it all in one place like that. I came up with a plot that Sam approved. He said not to worry too much about getting all the details of

MSMM Jan. 1985 with Reasoner's "The Elephant's Graveyard"

Fort Worth Nights (The Book Place, 2012) collects all the Cody short stories and adds a new one: "Assisted Dying"

character and setting down, that he could always polish up the manuscript if he needed to. So I wrote the story, sent it in, and in a pretty short time got a check for $300, my biggest payday so far as a writer. I didn't hear anything else about the story until I got the November 1978 issue and found a house ad in it for the next issue, featuring the Mike Shayne story "Death in Xanadu" (my title) by James M. Reasoner. What? Not by Brett Halliday? When somebody was putting together that ad, they forgot to change the by-line, the only time I'm aware of that ever happening in the magazine. Then, the next month, I found copies of the December 1978 issue at a newsstand in downtown Corpus Christi, Texas (we were staying in a nearby town on a short vacation over the Thanksgiving holiday) and there was my Shayne story, with a striking cover and the Brett Halliday name on it. That was the first time I'd ever been published under a housename. And when I went through the story itself, looking to see how Sam had "polished it up", as far as I could tell he changed one word in the manuscript. I've always been really proud of nailing the characters and style that well the first time out.

TDE: During the seven years (1978–1984) you wrote Mike Shayne stories as Brett Halliday, the magazine went through several Editors. Sam Merwin, Jr. was at the helm in 1978, then Larry Shaw took over for a short period in 1979, and finally Charles Fritch took over until the magazine ended in 1985. How did you manage the transition?

JR: Sam Merwin wanted me to do short outlines for the stories so he would know what they were about and wouldn't schedule plots that were too similar back to back. He had other writers besides me doing the Shayne stories (including

MSMM Dec. 1978 with Reasoner's "Death in Xanadu"

himself), so he had to be careful about such things. But I don't recall him ever suggesting any changes in them and he never asked me to do rewrites. Larry Shaw was there for such a short time I never had any contact with him at all. I'm sure I would have if he had stayed around, but it didn't work out that way.

Now, Charles E. Fritch had been there all along while I was selling to the magazine, working as an assistant editor for Sam and then for Larry Shaw, so when Shaw left it was a pretty seamless transition to Chuck, as far as I could tell. Chuck and I got along great. I believe I sent him an outline or two, which he approved, but then he said that as far as he was concerned, I could write all the Shayne stories if I wanted to. And if I did, he wouldn't need outlines anymore, since he figured I wouldn't write two in a row that were too similar. I jumped at the chance for the regular work. $300 a month, month in and month out, was great. We were able to buy a used van after saving up that Mike Shayne money for a while. Having a regular writing job was also valuable training for me. I learned the sort of self-discipline I needed to come up with a workable plot and

Complete In the Next Issue—

DEATH IN XANADU

The Thrilling New MIKE SHAYNE Short Novel

by JAMES M. REASONER

When a buccaneering young newspaper mogul's life is threatened, the Miami redhead is reluctant to take the case—not because of a lack of suspects but because there are too many. In short order, Shayne finds himself a potential target for the mysterious marksman and is forced to finding a solution to save his own skin.

Advertisement for Reasoner's "Death in Xanadu" from *MSMM* Nov. 1978

20,000 words month after month. Of course, after a while when I'd gotten the hang of it, I actually did more than that. I remember one month I wrote three Shayne stories back to back, which got me ahead enough on the schedule that I had time to write some novel proposals. Chuck was great to work with, never gave me trouble on the stories, and never seemed to mind too much when I called him to complain that the publisher was getting slower and slower on the checks. He's the only one of the three *MSMM* editors I ever spoke to on the phone.

As an aside, many years later I got Chuck's email address from a mutual friend and we made contact again and traded some stories about those days. He had been retired from writing and editing for a long time and worked for some state agency in California. I was sorry to hear when he passed away. He was a well-respected fantasy and science fiction writer who was also around the paperback and magazine business for a long time.

TDE: Was anyone from David Dresser's estate involved in reviewing your stories?

JR: Not that I'm aware of. I don't know what Dresser's role was early on in the magazine, but I don't think the estate did anything other than cash the checks for the licensing fee.

TDE: With the number of pages you contributed to *MSMM* every year, it must have been sad to see the magazine fold in 1985. How did you replace a major market like *MSMM* for your writing?

JR: After 1982, I didn't really write much for *MSMM* (a couple of short stories and one last Mike Shayne in '84), so the magazine's demise didn't mean much to me as a market. However, the publisher was so far behind in paying me for stories that when the magazine folded, he still owed me $242 (yes, I remember the total). So I wasn't happy about that. But I'd started writing less and less for the magazine as I began selling novels in the early Eighties and had even gotten Chuck Fritch to let me reduce the length of the Shayne stories to 10,000 words at times. So as a reader and fan, I was sorry to see *MSMM* go after it had had such a long run, but it folding didn't have much of an effect on my career . . . which cratered in '85 and '86 anyway, when I wasn't able to sell anything except a little ghostwriting work and some men's magazine stories.

TDE: Were there any stories you sold to *MSMM* that never saw print? What happened to them?

JR: I don't believe so. I think everything I sold them was published, if not always paid for.

TDE: In the Sept. 1979 issue of *MSMM*, Larry Shaw quoted your letter in which you asked, ". . . why none of the mystery magazines have a Letters to the Editor column." Shortly after Charles Fritch took over, a letter column, "Mike's Mail" started in January 1980 and appeared periodically from then on. Fritch also ran other short features like Minute Mysteries, Mike Shamus— and beginning in March 1981—a short-lived series on pulp characters by Michael Avallone, with artwork by Frank Hamilton. In September 1981, one reader wrote that he was buying the magazine solely for the pulp material. He closed with, "So get back to pulp-related material and make me want

MSMM August 1981 with Reasoner's "Midnight Wind"

MSMM February 1982 with Reasoner's "Doomsday Island"

to buy your magazine again." It's a shame he didn't "care for detective or mystery stories." He missed some of your Mike Shayne short novels like the Black Lotus series (Jan. 1981 [see page 82], Aug. 1981, and Feb. 1982) which remind me very much of heroic pulp fiction—including the fight scenes. What triggered the series and how did the stories, and the Black Lotus character, evolve?

JR: Chuck Fritch suggested that I create a recurring Oriental villainess for Shayne. Of course, this was nearly 40 years ago, in less enlightened times, and Chuck and I were both old enough to remember when such characters were staples of popular fiction. My first thought was that I wanted her to be the granddaughter of Fu Manchu, although I knew I could only hint around about that and not use any of Sax Rohmer's characters. I was a huge fan of the Seventies comic book *Master of Kung Fu*, though, which also featured a descendant of Fu Manchu, and this was my chance to do something similar.

Looking back on it now, I don't think I named the character well and should have done more with her, but the stories sure were fun to write at the time. By the time I wrote the final one, "Doomsday Island", the series had taken on a bit of a James Bond/*Man From U.N.C.L.E.* feeling. I even put a dedication on the manuscript to "Robert Hart Davis", the house-name that was used on all the U.N.C.L.E. digest magazines that Renown Publications also published. Chuck didn't run the dedication when the story appeared, though, which has always been a bit of a disappointment to me.

Black Lotus

- ☐ "Black Lotus" *MSMM* Jan. 1981
- ☐ "Death from the Sky" *MSMM* July 1981
- ☐ "Midnight Wind" *MSMM* Aug. 1981
- ☐ "Doomsday Island" *MSMM* Feb.1982

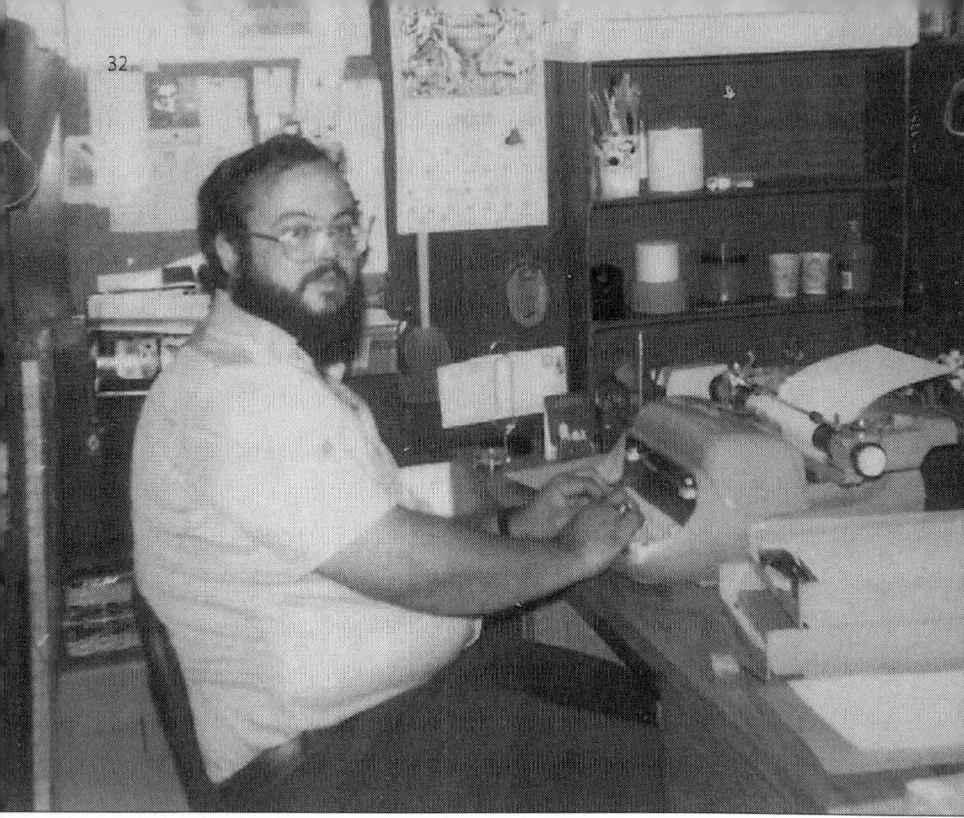

James Reasoner seated at his electric typewriter in the office where he wrote stories for *Mike Shayne Mystery Magazine*. Photo by Tom Johnson. c. 1981

I remember I hinted in one of the stories that Fu Manchu was still alive (without using the name, of course) and if I'd continued, I might have tried to bring him back under some other identity. That never happened, though.

I think there's a strong pulp influence running through most of my work, not just in the action scenes. I've read so many pulps, and so many paperbacks by writers who started out in the pulps, that I just can't help it! I love Robert E. Howard's boxing stories, so many of the fistfights I write have sort of the same feel to them. My gunfights are the same way, a little over the top, maybe, but with plenty of guns blazing and muzzle flame spurting and clouds of powdersmoke rolling. I like big, dramatic action scenes, and that goes straight back to the pulps. Now, from time to time I'll write some action that's pretty terse and understated because I think it works better in a particular scene, so I can handle it either way, but mostly I strive to have the action leaping right off the page.

TDE: Shayne takes a cruise with a bunch of mystery writers in "Killer's Cruise" (*MSMM* Sep. 1981). Several real authors are along for the ride—not ID'd by name, but through descriptive clues. I'm guessing the slender, distinguished college professor from Texas is Bill Crider, the man who wrote macabre suspense novels and taught martial arts is Joe Lansdale, the husband and wife writing team is you and

Livia Washburn, and the "fastest typewriter in the East" is Michael Avallone. What sparked the idea for this adventure? What did the authors say when they found out you planted them in the story?

JR: I'm going by memory here, but I think my friend Tom Johnson, who published the pulp fanzine *Echoes* and was a long-time fan of *MSMM* was in there as well. At one time Tom had a complete collection of *MSMM*, but I believe he may have sold it. You've identified the others accurately. I don't recall who came up with the idea for this story, but I think it was either Livia or myself. I don't remember anyone else suggesting it. It just seemed like a fun thing to do, and I've always enjoyed reading stories with little in-jokes like that. Everyone seemed to like it. At least, I don't recall anyone complaining!

TDE: Yes, a "Thomas Johnson" appears as the VP of Sanger Press in the story. In "Yesterday's Angel" (*MSMM* Sept. 1980), Shayne's deceased wife, Phyllis, is suddenly resurrected. Where did this one come from?

JR: When Sam Merwin asked me if I wanted to write a Shayne story, there was no deadline on it, so in addition to reading the Shayne bible he sent me, I took a couple of weeks to read, or in some cases re-read, the first dozen or so books in the series, just to really immerse myself in the characters and setting before I started writing. I really enjoyed the early books that featured Phyllis and thought it would be nice to bring her back someday, in some fashion. I also got the idea of coming up with a story that would fill in the gap between

MSMM September 1981 with Reasoner's "Killer's Cruise" Cover by Merle Keller

the novels *Murder Wears A Mummer's Mask* and *Blood on the Black Market*, because it's during that gap that Phyllis dies (Davis Dresser, the original Brett Halliday, having killed her off because he'd sold rights to the Mike Shayne character to the movies and Hollywood didn't want him to be married). These ideas lingered in my head as I continued to write Shayne stories, and eventually, after Chuck Fritch took over as editor of *MSMM*, I mentioned wanting to do a story set during World War II that would deal with Phyllis's death.

As an aside, let me say that my attitude in approaching the Shayne stories was time paradox be damned. The Shayne character from the Thirties and Forties was the same guy I was writing about in the Seventies and Eighties, and he hadn't aged much. Because of that, I tried to keep my stories relatively timeless. I wasn't always able to do

MSMM Oct. 1980 with Reasoner's "Mayhem in the Magic City" Cover by Tony Gleason

that, but when the plot required something more modern, I just didn't worry about it. I have no problem with suspension of disbelief when it comes to such things.

Anyway, when I said that about a World War II story to Chuck, he liked the idea and decided to devote an entire issue to historical mysteries, calling it a Crimes in Other Times special issue. Before I did the story dealing with Phyllis's death, though, I wanted to introduce her to the readers (some of whom might not have ever read those early novels) with the story that became "Yesterday's Angel". I didn't want to violate the continuity Dresser had established, so I had to come up with some other way to get Phyllis into the story. I wound up making it a sequel to *The Corpse Came Calling*, one of my favorites of the early novels. Looking back at it, I think I revealed too much of the novel's plot in my story, but I was still fairly new at the writing game back then. I believe I would handle it more skillfully now. But that said, I like those two Phyllis stories very much and the long-time fans of the series responded to them just the way I hoped. I remember Mike Avallone, who wrote a number of Shayne stories for *MSMM* himself, telling me how much he liked them. Having one of my own writing heroes say something like that to me was a mighty good feeling.

TDE: Your wife, Livia Washburn, is also a writer. When did you first meet and what was your first project together?

JR: Livia's older brother Bruce went all the way through school with me and was one of my best friends from first grade on. So I was always kind of aware of her. When Bruce and I were in college, we carpooled sometimes. I would stop by his house to pick him up and he was always running late, so while I was waiting for him I would talk to Livia and got to know her better that way. We started dating while I was in college and got married a year or so after I graduated.

I don't remember our first official project together. As I mentioned earlier, I had almost given up on the idea of writing, but Livia encouraged me to try again and really work at it. In those days, I was first-drafting everything in longhand, writing with a fountain pen in spiral notebooks. Livia would type up the stories when I was done with them, then I'd go over them and revise them, and she would type the final draft. In that intermediate stage, when she was working from my handwritten drafts, she would make suggestions

The Corpse Came Calling Dell 842 (reprint of Dell 324, 1942) Cover by Robert Schulz

MSMM September 1980 with Reasoner's "Yesterday's Angel" Cover by Bill Edwards

for things I could add or change. They always improved the stories, so after a while I told her, "Well, why don't you just go ahead and make those changes for me?" She had never really thought about being a writer, but that's how she discovered that she had a knack for it. Pretty soon she was plotting stories for me and writing her own. We collaborated on the historical romance novel *The Emerald Land* (published by Fawcett under the pseudonym Livia James, the only time we ever used that name). That was probably our first official collaboration. Since then, we've each contributed to nearly everything the other writes, whether it's an official collaboration or not. She's plotted and outlined many of my books without ever getting any credit for it, to the point that I don't really remember who did what.

TDE: I see that L.J. Washburn sold a good number of stories to *MSMM* too. In addition to writing, I read you two owned a bookstore at one time. What was that like?

JR: Looking at the list of stories Livia published in *MSMM*, I see now that "The Singer at Dawn" was actually our first official collaboration [*MSMM*, Oct. 1980]. That's a historical mystery featuring the Roman Emperor Claudius as the detective. She co-wrote a number of the Mike Shayne stories with me, and one of them, "A Cry in the Night" (November 1981), is almost entirely her work. Our styles aren't dramatically different, which is understandable since she got her start in writing by typing up and revising my stories. Which makes it easier for both of us to pinch-hit here and there on each other's books.

We got into the bookstore business because in the early Eighties we'd been trying to make a living as full-time writers and had struggled

MSMM November 1981 with Washburn's "A Cry in the Night"

at that. We started looking around for something that would give us some cash flow while still allowing time to write. My dad owned a business that sold and serviced TVs and appliances. I had worked for him for a while as office manager and part-time repairman, so he offered us some of the space in his building to start a bookstore in return for me running the office again. We set that up in early 1983. In '84, a friend of ours who had a used bookstore in Fort Worth decided to get out of the used book business and sold us his stock. We used it to open a second store, this one on the east side of Fort Worth. I ran it, while Livia took over running the original store, which she did until she got pregnant, and then my dad stepped in and ran it along with his own business. (I can't say enough good things about my dad, by the way.)

The problem is that while the used book business is great fun in many ways, it doesn't make much money. It took us three years to build up the Fort Worth store to the point it was actually turning a small but consistent profit. The original location in our hometown never did. Plus I had a 45-minute commute to the Fort Worth store every day. In February 1987, our lease was up on that store. I asked the landlord if he would let us stay there for another year to see if things continued to grow, but he refused. It was either sign another three-year lease or get out. So we got out. I'd started selling novels again after the drought of '84 and '85 and actually had enough writing work lined up for us to live on. We closed down both stores and were back to being full-time writers. We've never done anything else in the 32 years since then.

Looking back on it, there were a lot of things I enjoyed about the bookstore years, mostly the friends I made among my customers. Also, my friend Kerry Newcomb, a great Western and historical novelist, lived nearby and stopped in frequently, dropping off hamburgers and milkshakes and watching old B-Westerns with me on the little TV I had behind the counter. I continued writing all along, too, on an electric typewriter I had on a desk I had made from a few boards and some boxes of old Harlequin Romances. I was at the bookstore when Lyle Kenyon Engel called me and asked me to come to work for Book Creations Inc., and I wrote my first two Stagecoach Station books there. Those years were the low point of my writing career, but they were also when I started climbing out of that hole.

TDE: Although I've never run

a bookstore, it's appeal isn't so far removed from making up stories for a living. What does a typical day of writing look like for you?

JR: My process has evolved some over the years. Early on, when I was writing most of my digest stories (on a typewriter), I worked mostly at night, would start at ten or eleven o'clock and work until four or five in the morning. Having kids changed all that. My routine on a normal day is to read a little while having breakfast, check email and catch up on any business matters that need tending to, and get to the computer to write sometime between nine and ten o'clock in the morning. I usually start by editing and polishing the pages I did the day before, then plunge right into writing new ones. I take a break for lunch around one, maybe read some or deal with other emails, then it's back to the computer by two. I usually have enough done for the day between five and six o'clock in the afternoon. So we're talking six to eight hours a day of actual writing, depending on how fast it goes.

For a long time, the afternoons were more productive for me than the mornings. It was like I had to get some steam built up. For the past couple of years, though, I've noticed that I seem to get more done in the morning, then taper off in the afternoon. Maybe that's because I'm getting older, I don't know.

TDE: You've written hundreds of stories of varying lengths. When you get an idea, how do you decide whether it's a short story, or something longer?

JR: As it's worked out, that's never really been an issue with me. Starting out, I just wrote short

Under Outlaw Flags
The Book Place edition 2011

stories because I didn't think I was ready to tackle a novel. Since I started writing novels regularly, those are the kind of ideas I came up with, and I stopped writing short stories unless it was for a specific purpose, for example when someone asked me to contribute to an anthology. Now, there have been times when I set out to write a 5,000 word short story and it wound up being a 15,000 word novella, but that's not exactly the same thing.

There was one case where I thought a science fiction novella I wrote could work as the opening section of a novel. I wasn't going to do the rest of the book myself, though. Bill Crider was going to take it and carry the story on from where I'd left off. He wrote an outline for a full-length novel using that idea, but that was as far as the project ever got.

TDE: Seems you've written

Dust Devils
The Book Place edition 2011

Tractor Girl
The Book Place edition 2011

pretty much every genre there is, with detective and western fiction holding the lead. What draws you to these genres?

JR: I've always enjoyed adventure fiction, no matter what the genre, but I think I became a fan of mysteries and Westerns early on because that's what I had available to me at the bookmobile. Those sections were where I wound up most Saturday mornings. And science fiction, too, although to a lesser extent. Even before I was reading much, the earliest TV shows I remember watching are Westerns: *The Lone Ranger*, *Gunsmoke*, *Have Gun Will Travel*, movies with Roy Rogers, Gene Autry, and William Boyd as Hopalong Cassidy.

I agree for the most part with the critical theories that link detective heroes with cowboys, the business about them being loners with guns and setting out to right wrongs and deliver justice. For me, though, the appeal is primarily about the action and the pace. As a reader, I want to be so caught up in the story that I can't turn the pages fast enough, and that's what I try to deliver as a writer.

Of course, liking to read just about every type of fiction means that I've wanted to write every type of fiction. I can't imagine writing the same genre over and over, just as I can't imagine reading the same one all the time.

TDE: What's your process for developing an idea into a finished piece?

JR: I've never outlined short stories, although I do like to have a fairly complete mental picture before I start writing. So I guess in a way I do outline, it's just in my head. I just wrote a short story for an anthology, and while I knew the opening and the middle part, I didn't know how it was going to end. So when I reached that point, I had to stop and let it percolate overnight, as I told Livia. (I don't know if coffee pots still percolate, but I'm old enough to remember when they did.) When I do that, I don't think about the problem directly, just keep it in the back of my mind, and then the solution comes to me, usually within a day or two.

With novels, I've used every method from long, detailed outlines including character sketches, a chapter-by-chapter breakdown, and even some bits of dialogue, to no outline at all and just a vague idea of what the plot will be. How I proceed depends on what the publisher wants and how much time I have for the project. Most of the time these days I write a synopsis of the book that runs five to ten pages and includes enough of the plot that I won't wander off into dead ends. That's proven to be a good process for me. If something occurs to me that's not in the outline, I'll make notes at the very end of the manuscript file so I won't forget, then delete them when I've written that part of the book.

TDE: Do you work on multiple stories at the same time?

JR: Very rarely, and then only as a last resort, usually due to some sort of scheduling glitch on my part. I've sometimes started a story, reached a point where I wasn't sure what to do with it, and put it aside to come back to it weeks, months, or in one case, years later and finish it. But that's not quite the same thing. I've known quite a few writers who routinely work on one project in the morning and a different one in the afternoon, but I'm not sure my brain could keep up with that on a regular basis.

TDE: With as much as you've written, how do you keep your work fresh? How do you challenge yourself to improve and explore new territory?

Wind River Book Seven *Ransom Valley*
The Book Place edition 2012

JR: I'm always on the lookout for the chance to write something different from what I've written before. After so many years and so many books, that's not easy, because sometimes I really do feel like I've written it all.

But of course I haven't. There are always new angles to explore, sometimes a particular plot twist or setting that I've never used before. Working with those is always rewarding.

I also try to never stop learning, as far as the craft of writing goes. If some other writer says, "I always do so-and-so" or "I never do so-and-so", I take a look at it and ask myself if such an approach could apply to my work. Most of the time, I'll give it a try and see. It usually doesn't take me long to figure out if something works for me.

Then there are the purely me-

Redemption Book One *Redemption, Kansas*
Berkley reissue 2011

chanical things, like playing with the font in Word. (I'll bet other writers do this, too.) I'll change fonts, bump the size up or down, change the page layout, anything for a bit of novelty. Not long ago I changed the page color to a light tan and arranged the text in double, justified columns. In other words, I made the display look as much like a page in a pulp magazine as I could. And then I wrote with it that way for a few days before going back to more standard formatting. I kept that colored background, though, because I found that it's easier on my eyes. I'll change it back to the normal style before I send the manuscript in.

TDE: Are there any particular stories or books you recommend to folks who are hearing about your work for the first time?

JR: My favorite of my books is *Under Outlaw Flags*, which is part Western, part World War I novel. I really like the voice in that one. My hardboiled crime novels *Dust Devils* and *Tractor Girl* are about as good as I can write in that genre, I think. For traditional Westerns, I'd recommend the Wind River series I wrote with Livia and the Redemption, Kansas series, the first one of which won the Peacemaker Award from Western Fictioneers for Best Novel.

TDE: When did you start Rough Edges Press? Who does what in the ongoing and special tasks that keep its wheels turning?

JR: The first Rough Edges Press book was *Blazing Trails and Western Tales* by Charles Boeckman in 2014. It's a collection of some of his stories from the Western pulps. Charles and I had gotten to know each other through the WesternPulps Yahoo Group. For a long time, I'd wanted to get involved in reprinting stories from the pulps, and this seemed like a perfect opportunity. Of course, it became a lot more than that (as things have a way of doing), and I wound up reprinting quite a few books by friends of mine and also publishing a considerable number of original titles, including some science fiction anthologies that produced an award-winner and several stories that were reprinted in a Best of the Year volume.

Livia does as much or more of the work than I do, handling all the covers, all the formatting for the print editions, and some of the formatting for the ebook editions. It would be impossible for me to do all that work, so Rough Edges Press wouldn't exist without her, no doubt about that. Mostly I just edit the books and do a little ebook formatting here and there.

TDE: As this interview winds up, it's late March 2019. Of course, readers can keep up on your projects via your blog <jamesreasoner.blogspot.com> and website <roughedges-press.com>, but what are you working on right now and what's coming up for the remainder of the year?

JR: Most of my work is ghostwriting these days, so I can't claim it. But I'm writing a frontier historical novel right now and have a contemporary thriller and four or five Westerns coming up later in the year. Under my own name, I have a story in the anthology *At Home in the Dark*, edited by Lawrence Block, and I've done a story for an anthology edited by Rick Ollerman that will be out in the fall of 2019, in conjunction with Bouchercon. My intention is to slow down on the ghostwriting in the next year or so and write more novels and stories under my name. I have a bunch of ideas ready to go!

At Home in the Dark Independent 2019
edited by Lawrence Block

All Mystery
Dell Publishing Co., Inc. New York
One issue
October–December 1950
5-1/2″ x 7-5/8″
160 pages
25¢ cover price

All Mystery Cover by Bob Stanley

When is a Digest Not a Digest?

Article by Ward Smith

Size matters—of course—but so does the way one presents the contents.

From about 1943 until 1947 the United States Government printed and gave away (yes, free) more than 122 million copies of books produced in what was named Armed Services Editions (ASEs). These compact publications were handed out to servicemen and women as part of what was described as a World War II literacy program.

Were these funny little books, printed on cheap newsprint with paper wraps, truly digests? In size they could be said to fit the criteria, most being 5½ inches to 6½ inches on one side and varying from 3⅞ inches to 4½ inches along the other axis. The distinguishing feature is that the short measurement was the side that was bound. In other words, these books could be said to be *digests lying on their side.*

Another specific descriptor of these books, as shown in the illustrations, is their labeling as "This is the Complete book—Not a Digest." This applied to almost all the published ASEs. In this respect, the word digest referred to edited and shortened versions of the original, as applied most prominently to many articles (and books) reprinted in *Reader's Digest* magazine. A few ASEs were noted as abridged (shortened).

"Digest," as a descriptor of size apparently began with—and was

874
RAMROD
A WESTERN BY
LUKE SHORT
RAMROD
LUKE SHORT
Overseas edition for the Armed Forces. Distributed by the Special Services Division, A.S.F., for the Army, and by the Bureau of Naval Personnel for the Navy. U. S. Government property. Not for sale. Published by Editions for the Armed Services, Inc., a non-profit organization established by the Council on Books in Wartime.
ARMED SERVICES EDITION
THIS IS THE COMPLETE BOOK—NOT A DIGEST

1. HOW I CAME TO MONTANA

PEOPLE WHO KNOW ME often talk as though I was from Texas. That is not correct. I was born at Cranwich Hall, Cranwich, County of Norfolk, England, December 17, 1860. But I came to Montana with a herd of Texas cattle in 1883.

That is where they get the idea that I am a Texan. All this part of Montana east of the mountains was settled by Texans who came here with the cattle, and so was Wyoming, and parts of Colorado and New Mexico, and the western half of the Dakotas, and even Nebraska before the farmers run them out. A lot of farmers and businessmen came in here after the cowpunchers, and there were a few other people who got here first. But the Texas cowboy's mode of speech and dress and actions set the style for all the range country. And his influence is not dead yet.

For a long time I have wanted to write a history of the cattle range and of the movement of the cattle as they were gradually pushed north over the Texas trail. I have read plenty of histories of the trail, written by other men who went over it, that are entirely accurate as to facts, but they are not told right. They are like these cowboy songs I have seen in books and heard over the radio, that are all fixed up and not the way we used to sing them at all. Other old-timers have told all about stampedes and swimming rivers and what a terrible time we had, but

7

indeed named for—*Reader's Digest*, which began in 1922. Some of the famous digests that followed were *TV Guide*, from 1953–2005, *Bird Watcher's Digest* begun in 1978, and the restaurant freebie *CoffeeHouse Digest*. This is not to mention the many mystery magazines, such as *Ellery Queen's Mystery Magazine*, and a slew of science-fiction and fantasy publications since the 1940s.

Digest-size magazines are smaller than conventional or "journal size" periodicals, although they

are larger in general than standard "paperback" books. The word "digest," as used to denote page size, often ranges from 14 by 21 cm (5½ x 8¼ inches) to as small as 14 by 19 cm (5½ x 7½ inches). A few digests measure 13.65 by 21.27 cm (5⅜ x 8⅜ inches). Printing press sheet sizes gave rise to these dimensions, sometimes called "catalog size." When introduced they were viewed as easy for people to carry around.

One of the sources I researched said that librarians kicked off the effort to supply reading material to the troops shortly after the attack on Pearl Harbor. While some 10 million books were donated to that cause, the size and weight of some books made shipping—especially overseas—prohibitive.

That's when a number of publishers got together to form the Council on Books in Wartime. Their solution was to print small, lightweight editions in a wide, two-column-per-page, "easy to read" format. These small paper-wrapped books were printed in small type to provide more words per page. They were usually stapled rather than simply glued. The idea at the time was that a GI could carry the book in a pocket (thus probably violating military uniform regulations) or stuff the book into a pack.

Printing costs were kept low—mere pennies per copy!—and authors and publishers divided the royalties, which amounted to a cent per copy. When you consider the many millions of copies, you can see that costs remained very low for the overall program.

As is clear in the accompanying illustrations, many ASEs reproduced the front dust jacket of the original publisher's edition. Many, perhaps most, ASEs were near-simultaneous duplicates of full-sized first editions. This brought the latest works to the attention of military personnel and is said to have thereby enhanced the literacy rate of Americans.

DRACULA ***by Bram Stoker***

For sheer, stalking, horrendous terror there is no match for *Dracula* in the English language. It has made millions of hardened mystery-readers and avid movie fans squirm with dread. But few people seem to know anything about the author—"Oh yes, Stoker, wasn't he the guy who wrote *Dracula?*" So here is the best chance to tell you something about him.

Bram Stoker was born in Dublin nearly a hundred years ago. He was a sickly child and could not walk until he was seven. Instead he lay on his back and did a good deal of thinking. However, before he was twenty, he had staged a comeback, and was considered the athletic champion of Dublin University

Ten dreary years as a civil servant were followed by experience as a journalist, a barrister, and as the manager of the famous actor, Henry Irving. With Irving, he toured America and wrote fifty letters a day. Subsequently, he was on the literary staff of the London *Telegraph*. Though he wrote other novels, *Dracula* is certainly his best-known.

This special edition of Dracula *by Bram Stoker has been made available to the Armed Forces of the United States through an arrangement with the original publisher, Doubleday, Doran and Co., Inc., New York.*

Editions for the Armed Services, Inc., a non-profit organization established by the Council on Books in Wartime

These compact books were not just fiction. Science, biography, sports, etc., were represented in the overall collection. But in addition to current works of fiction, classics by such authors as Mark Twain and H.G. Wells were printed as ASEs. There were also made-up editions of short story collections, poetry, essays, and even scripts from broadcasted radio plays. Contemporary writers such as William Faulkner, C.S. Forester, Erle Stanley Gardner, Ngaio Marsh, John O'Hara, Thorne Smith, and Philip Wylie were represented. Thus, G.I. readers were kept abreast of the tops in literary achievement. But there was even an ASE book dedicated to *Superman*!

The records show there were 1,324 books printed *en toto*, of which 99 were reprints of earlier ASE titles and 1,225 were unique to the publishing effort. Each book was identified with a unique number printed on the upper left front cover, as shown in the illustration. In spite of the quality of paper used, the books proved quite durable during the war. However, their handling and storage under difficult wartime conditions eventually took a toll, and most remaining copies available on the resale market are in only "fair" to "about good" condition.

There is a complete set of ASEs at the Library of Congress. Some colleges, such as Notre Dame and the University of South Carolina have nearly complete sets. Collectors sets are incomplete, with the exception of one person who has a complete run of all 1,324 books.

So, were the Armed Services Editions digests?

Yes. No. Whatever!

Ward Smith is a pen name used by a collector of vintage books with paper wraps, including Armed Services Editions, original Pocket Books, Dell "Mapbacks," and some early wartime digests.

Startling Mystery Stories No. 1 Summer 1966 Cover by Hubert Carter

Series Overview by Peter Enfantino

"In the publishing business, it takes many months after an issue has gone off sale before one can tell what happened, good or bad. If your letters and ballots are any indication, then our first issue did well—"

–Robert A.W. Lowndes, *Startling Mystery Stories* No. 3, page 116

Way back in *TDE* No. 5, I covered the 36 issues of the Robert A.W. Lowndes-edited *Magazine of Horror*. *MOH* had a sister publication, *Startling Mystery Stories*, which ran for 18 issues from 1966 through 1971. *SMS* is perhaps most famous for running Stephen King's first two professional sales, but it also had several other highlights to recommend it to collectors. Copies of the non-King issues can be had relatively cheap on eBay (a glance turns up several for less than 20 bucks a pop), if this quick peek whets your appetite.

"The big news this time," began Robert A. W. Lowndes in the letters page of *Magazine of Horror* No. 13, "is the inauguration of our companion magazine, *Startling Mystery Stories*. While this publication is restricted to mystery tales, we are stressing the eerie, bizarre, and strange type of mystery, rather than the mundane crime story (however excellent) to be found in other magazines of this caliber. Thus you will find not a few authors and types of story quite in line with some of the content of *Magazine of Horror*."

As with *MOH*, RAWL managed to make *SMS* more like a fan club newsletter (tantamount to a gathering in the tree house to compare new comic book purchases) than a "mainstream publication." Of course, this newsletter was flavored with lots of prime reprints and several strong pieces of original fiction.

No. 1 Summer 1966 130 pgs 50¢

Initially, *Startling Mystery Stories* contained no "Editor's Page" as in *Magazine of Horror*. There's simply an introduction and in that introduction, editor Robert A. W. Lowndes tells us a little bit about each story and lets us know what we can expect in *SMS*. "Village of the Dead" was not only the first story in the long-running Simon Ark series, but it was also the first published Edward D. Hoch story. Way back in *The Scream Factory* No. 18 (Autumn 1996), Ed Hoch was nice enough to write a piece for us on the history of Simon (including a complete bibliography of Ark appearances). RAWL mentions that the Derleth story will appear in an upcoming hardcover titled *Harrigan's Files*. That book didn't appear until 1975 (published by Arkham House). "The Mansion of Unholy Magic" is a Jules de Grandin story. Strangely, RAWL picks a story years into the series (it began in *Weird Tales* in 1925) rather than one of the first. Hubert Carter designed the logo for SMS and *Famous Science Fiction* and did the cover for *SMS* No. 1.

SMS No. 1 Contents

(4) "Village of the Dead" by Edward D. Hoch (7500 words) from *Famous Detective Stories* Dec. 1955
(3) "House of the Hatchet" by Robert Bloch (7000 words) from *Weird Tales* Jan. 1941
(5) "The Off-Season" by Gerald W. Page (3100 words)*
(6) "The Tell-Tale Heart" by Edgar Allan Poe (2500 words) uncredited source
(2) "The Lurking Fear" by H. P. Lovecraft (9750 words) from *Home Brew* Jan. 1923
(7) "The Awful Injustice" by S. B. H. Hurst (4500 words) from *Strange Tales* Sep.1931
(8) "Ferguson's Capsules" by August Derleth (4000 words)*
(1) "The Mansion of Unholy Magic" by Seabury Quinn (16,000 words) from *Weird Tales* Oct. 1933

No. 2 Fall 1966 130 pgs 50¢

In his intro, RAWL reveals that ten of Quinn's de Grandin tales are "off-limits" as they appear in a then-new hardcover collection, *The Phantom Fighter* (Mycroft & Moran), which is reviewed in the "Books" section. Also reviewed is the science fiction anthology, *Strange Signposts*, edited by Roger Elwood and Sam Moscowitz. For some reason, RAWL skips the second Simon Ark story, "The Hoofs of Satan" (*Famous Detective Stories* Feb. 1956), and instead publishes the third in the chronology. The first in a series of eight stories starring the titular bad guy, "Doctor Satan" was Paul Ernst's (and *Weird Tales*') attempt to create a popular pulp character ala Doc Savage or The Spider. The difference in this case, of course, was that the Doctor was a villain. RAWL got around to reprinting six of the eight stories. Bob Weinberg reprinted

Key to Contents List Notations

() Readers' story preference ranks are listed in parentheses. Ballot ranks appeared in "The Reckoning," in the issue following the stories' appearance.
* indicates a story original to *Startling Mystery Stories*
Word counts (listed in parentheses) are estimates based on actual word counts of two full-page sample columns. (Each ran approximately 250 words.)
The original appearance of each reprint is noted when known.

five of the stories (including the two RAWL didn't get to) in *Pulp Classics* No. 6 (1974). Terry Carr and Ted White were both respected editors and anthologists. White wrote one of my favorite comic book novels, *The Great Gold Steal* (Bantam, 1968), starring Captain America. He also edited *F&SF*, *Amazing*, and *Fantastic* in the 1960s and 70s. Carr edited *The Best Science Fiction of the Year* anthology from 1972 through 1987 and 17 volumes of *Universe*, an annual anthology of new SF. Carr and White were the co-authors of *Invasion from 2500* (Monarch, 1964) a pulpish SF novel with a fabulous cover. The first installment of "The Cauldron," *Startling Mystery*'s answer to *MOH*'s "It Is Written." In the inaugural, RAWL gives bios of each of the authors that appear in this issue. Letter writers include Robert Silverberg and Edward D. Hoch.

Startling Mystery Stories No. 2 Fall 1966
Cover by Carl Kidwell

SMS 2 Contents

(1) "The House of Horror" by Seabury Quinn (9250 words) from *Weird Tales* Jul. 1926
(5) "The Men in Black" by John Brunner (4250 words)*
(7) "The Strange Case of Pascal" by Roger Eugene Ulmer (2500 words) from *Weird Tales* Jun. 1926
(6) "The Witch is Dead" by Edward D. Hoch (8500 words) from *Famous Detective Stories* Apr. 1956
(2) "Doctor Satan" by Paul Ernst (11,250 words) from *Weird Tales* Aug. 1935
(3) "The Secret of the City" by Terry Carr and Ted White (3500 words)*
(4) "The Scourge of B'Moth" by Bertram Russell (13,750 words) from *Weird Tales* May 1929

No. 3 Winter 1966/67 130 pgs 50¢

Finally establishing an "Editor's Page," RAWL debates the merits of updating outdated stories (he's pretty much against it). Gaston Leroux, of course, is best known for his novel, *The Phantom of the Opera*. In his author bios, Lowndes mistakenly credits Lon Chaney with two versions of *The Phantom*. He claims he saw a "talking" version of the 1925 classic (save Chaney speaking himself). I suspect this was either misremembering or some kind of revival. Probably the former. In the book section, RAWL reviews *Colonel Markesan and Less Pleasant People* by August Derleth. "The Door of Doom" is illustrated by H.W. Wesso. I could find only one other story written by Ralph E. Hayes ("Yesterday's 7000 Years" in *Adam* Sep. 1963), even though RAWL mentions, in the author bio, that Hayes is a mystery and detective story writer. Lowndes mentions that Hayes would have appeared in the fourth issue of *Chase* had it been published. I wonder if this is the same Ralph Hayes who would go on to author several novels in the 1970s, including the five-novel

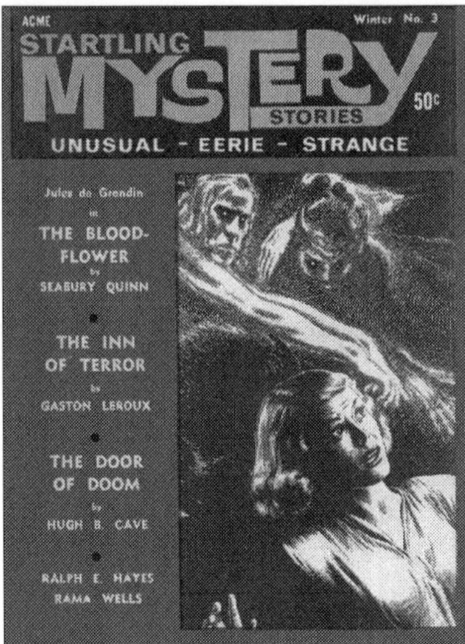

Startling Mystery Stories No. 3 Winter 1966/67
Cover by Virgil Finlay

Startling Mystery Stories No. 4 Spring 1967
Cover by Virgil Finlay

series "The Hunter" for Leisure. In his bio, RAWL claims that Rama Wells "is well known for non-fiction under a different name, which we are constrained not to divulge; this is his first appearance with us, but he is reticent about saying whether it is also his first fiction sale." Well, evidently "Rama" is still reticent or maybe still relatively unknown under his real name as I can find no trace of Rama after this issue. It was his only Health Knowledge appearance. The Quinn story is a Jules de Grandin adventure (the 11th of the 93 to be published in *Weird Tales*). Letter writers in "The Cauldron" include Ed Wood and Mike Ashley.

SMS No. 3 Contents

(1) "The Inn of Terror"
by Gaston Leroux (10,250 words)
from *Weird Tales* Aug. 1929
(5) "The Other" by Robert A. W. Lowndes
(1750 words) from *Stirring Science Stories* Apr. 1941
(4) "The Door of Doom"
by Hugh B. Cave (11,750 words)
from *Strange Tales* Jan. 1932
(3) "A Matter of Breeding" by Ralph E. Hayes
(4000 words)*
(6) "Esmerelda" by Rama Wells (4250 words)*
(7) "The Trial for Murder"
by Charles Collins & Charles Dickens
(5000 words) uncredited source
(2) "The Blood-Flower" by Seabury Quinn
(10,750 words) from *Weird Tales* Mar. 1927

No. 4 Spring 1967 130 pgs 50¢

In "The Editor's Page," RAWL responds to a reader who requests a new department for stories by "budding writers of today." In keeping with stuffing *SMS* with series characters, Lowndes adds August Derleth's poor man's Sherlock Holmes, Solar Pons to his roster. For more info on the weird and potholed history of the Robert E. Howard story, see my notes for *MOH* No. 13 [*TDE5* pg 130]. In the body of the story, RAWL reprints Harry Bates' letter to Robert E. Howard explaining the cancellation of *Strange Tales* and thus the return of the story to Howard (dated October 4, 1932).

Also reprinted is the first page of the returned manuscript including Bates' notes and corrections. A fascinating bit of history. *Black Medicine* by Arthur J. Burks is reviewed in "Books." In "The Cauldron," a fan meeting with August Derleth (who spoke on Solar Pons) is detailed. Writing in is Ted White and Glenn Lord. Author bios are also included.

SMS No. 4 Contents

(4) "The Adventure of the Tottenham Werewolf" by August Derleth (9250 words) from *The Memoirs of Solar Pons*
(2) "The Secret of Lost Valley" by Robert E. Howard (9750 words)*
(3) "Medium for Justice" by Victor Rousseau (8250 words) from *Ghost Stories* Jul. 1928, originally as "The Blackest Magic of All"
(5) "Si Urag of the Tail" by Oscar Cook (7000 words) from *Weird Tales* Jul. 1926
(6) "The Temptation of Harringay" by H. G. Wells (2500 words) from *The Stolen Bacillus and Others*
(1) "The Tenants of Broussac" by Seabury Quinn (14,500 words) from *Weird Tales* Dec. 1925

Startling Mystery Stories No. 5 Summer 1967
Cover by Virgil Finlay

No. 5 Summer 1967 130 pgs 50¢

On The Editor's Page, RAWL continues the debate over a "new writer's" department. "A Game of Chess" comes with an introduction by Sam Moskowitz. The Quinn story (another de Grandin) is illustrated twice (once by Rankin, while the other is not identified). In his intro to the story, RAWL informs us that "Behind the Curtain" would have run in *Chase*. The story illustration is uncredited. "The Man from Nowhere" is a Simon Ark story. Another uncredited illo for "The Darkness on Fifth Avenue." *Deep Waters* by William Hope Hodgson is reviewed in the "Books" section. In "The Cauldron," RAWL discusses Robert E. Howard's enduring popularity and Solar Pons' non-horrific elements (which have raised eyebrows among readers who want only "weird fiction"). Marvin Jones writes in from Los Angeles to beat down RAWL for the *Phantom of the Opera* inaccuracies in the last issue. Thanks for backing me up, Marv. Also writing in is Mike Ashley.

SMS 5 Contents

(3) "The Gods of East and West" by Seabury Quinn (13,500 words) from *Weird Tales* Jan. 1928
(5) "The Council" / "The House" (verse) by Robert A. W. Lowndes
(6) "Behind the Curtain" by Leslie Jones (2000 words)*
(1) "A Game of Chess" by Robert Barr (5500 words) from *Pearson's Magazine* Mar. 1900
(4) "The Man From Nowhere" by Edward D. Hoch (6750 words) from *Famous Detective Stories* Jun. 1956
(2) "The Darkness on Fifth Avenue" by Murray Leinster (23,250 words) from *Argosy* Nov. 30, 1929

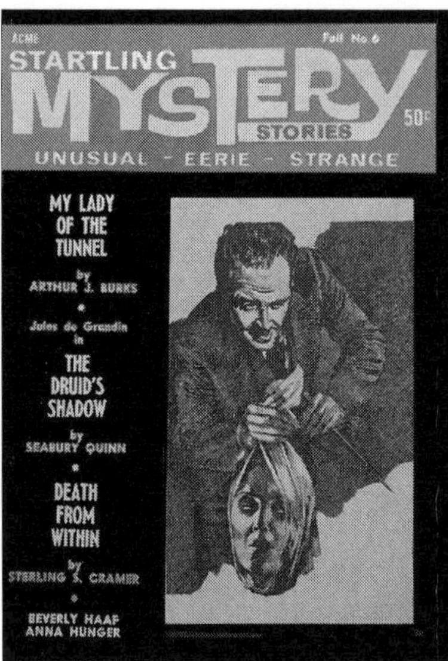

Startling Mystery Stories No. 6 Fall 1967
Cover by Virgil Finlay

No. 6 Fall 1967 130 pgs 50¢

This is, of course, one of the two Holy Grails for collectors looking to complete their set of *Startling Mystery* (or their collection of Stephen King first appearances, for that matter). At one point in time, there were several copies of the issue on sale on abebooks.com with prices ranging from $750–1500. It's Stephen King's first pro sale, which is why the bounty is so high. King actually had one other story appear before this ("I Was a Teenage Grave-Robber" in *Comics Review,* which was reprinted as "In a Half-World of Terror" in Marv Wolfman's fanzine, *Stories of Suspense* No. 2, 1965) but good luck finding a copy of that. *SMS* No. 6 is around, but you'll pay a lot of money for it. For history's sake, here's RAWL's intro to "The Glass Floor":

> *"Stephen King has been sending us stories for some time, and we returned one of them most reluctantly, since it would be far too long before we could use it, due to its length. But patience may yet bring him his due reward on that tale; meanwhile, here is a chiller whose length allowed us to get it into print much sooner."*

Readers were indifferent to the future superstar though, as they voted "The Glass Floor" 5th out of 7 stories in "The Reckoning" the following issue. King would have been about 20 years old at this time. I'm not sure if it's laziness on RAWL's part, but there seems to be a plethora of uncredited illustrations lately. Another one appears with "My Lady of the Tunnel." However, a badly reproduced illustration credited to Hugh Rankin appears for "The Druid's Shadow." In "The Cauldron," RAWL relates that he has won the Praed Penny Award from the Praed Street Irregulars for reprinting "The Adventure of the Tottenham Werewolf" back in *SMS* No. 4. The award was accepted at the "Annual PSI dinner" by Forrest J. Ackerman. Others in attendance were Vincent Starrett and Robert Bloch. An Index to Volume One also appears.

SMS No. 6 Contents

(2) "My Lady of the Tunnel" by Arthur J. Burks (7250 words) from *Astounding* Nov. 1933
(5) "The Glass Floor" by Stephen King (3250 words)*
"Death from Within" by Sterling S. Cramer (10,750 words) from *Wonder Stories* Jun. 1935
(6) "A Vision" (verse)* by Robert E. Howard
(7) "Aim for Perfection" by Beverly Haaf (2500 words)*
(3) "The Dark Castle" by Marion Brandon (5500 words) from *Strange Tales* Sep. 1931
(4) "Dona Diabla" by Anna Hunger (5000 words)*
(1) "The Druid's Shadow" by Seabury Quinn

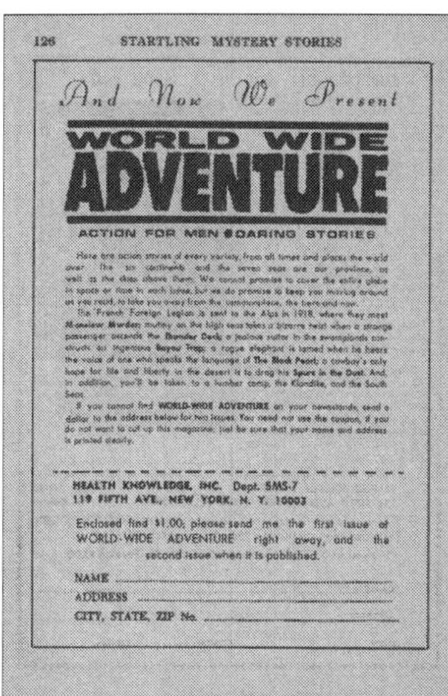

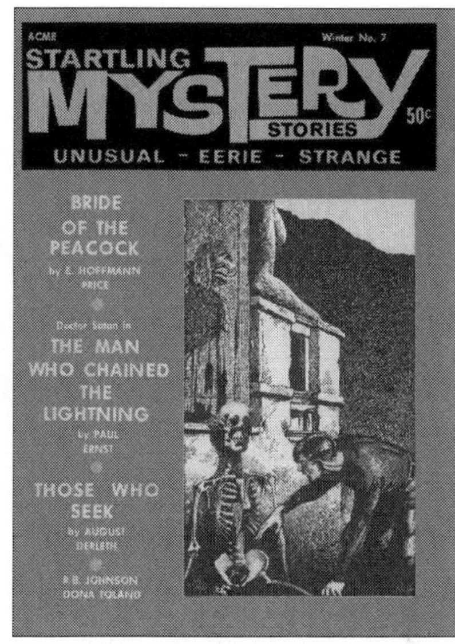

Startling Mystery Stories No. 7 Winter 1967/68 Left: Advertisement for *World Wide Adventure.* Right: Cover by Virgil Finlay

(14,500 words) from *Weird Tales* Oct. 1930

No. 7 Winter 1967/68 130 pgs 50¢

On "The Editor's Page," Robert A. W. Lowndes announces that they are finally taking subscription orders for *SMS*. "The Bride of the Peacock" features E. Hoffman Price's Pierre D'Artois character, "a Frenchman who seems to have a propensity for getting involved with Devil worshippers of the Persian variety" according to RAWL. The story is illustrated by T. Wyatt Nelson. "Those Who Seek" is illustrated by Joseph Doolin. In his intro to "The Man Who Chained . . .", RAWL explains why Farnsworth Wright ran the Doctor Satan series in *Weird Tales*. In "The Cauldron," RAWL mentions a fanzine by Paul J. Willis called *Anubis*. The first ad is run for Health Knowledge's new digest, *World Wide Adventure*. *WWA* was comprised predominately of reprints from *Adventure* and *Argosy* and lasted seven issues.

SMS No. 7 Contents

(1) "The Bride of the Peacock" by E. Hoffman Price (22,500 words) from *Weird Tales* Aug. 1932
(5) "Nice Old House" by Dona Tolson (2000 words)*
(2) "Those Who Seek" by August Derleth (4750 words) from *Weird Tales* Jan. 1932
(4) "John Bartine's Watch" by Ambrose Bierce (2500 words) from *Can Such Things Be?*
(6) "The Pet of Mrs. Lilith" by Robert Barbour Johnson (6500 words) from *Mystic* Jan. 1954
(3) "The Man Who Chained the Lightning" by Paul Ernst (11,750 words) from *Weird Tales* Sep. 1935

No. 8 Spring 1968 130 pgs 50¢

With this issue, *SMS* changes its format from two columns to one (except for the Haywood story). Jules de Grandin appears in "The White Lady." The story is presented with illos (uncredited) of de Grandin and his partner, Dr. Samuel Trow-

Startling Mystery Stories No. 8 Spring 1968
Cover by Virgil Finlay

Startling Mystery Stories No. 9 Summer 1968
Cover by Virgil Finlay

bridge. Sam Moskowitz introduces the Haywood story, which includes illustrations by Joseph Doolin. Clark Ashton Smith's "The Return of the Sorcerer" is illustrated by pulp legend Rafael de Soto (responsible for many classic *Black Mask* covers). Jay Tyler was a pseudonym used by RAWL. In "The Cauldron," RAWL discusses the difference between the stories included in *MOH* and *SMS*. Letter writer Ron Smith comments: "The Glass Floor" (in *SMS* No. 6, written by Stephen King) was interesting and rather shocking. King is a very promising young writer and I'm sorry you had to send back his longer tale. It would have been extremely interesting to see how he stood up in a longer story" (I wonder if Mr. Smith felt the same after reading King's behemoth, *The Stand*). To which RAWL replies: "Author King is cordially invited to re-submit the story I had to return, due to length, if it is not over 6000 words!" I've no idea if the story discussed was "The Reaper's Image," which was published a year later in *SMS* No. 12 (and did run under 6000 words).

SMS No. 8 Contents

(2) "The White Lady of the Orphanage" by Seabury Quinn (10,250 words) from *Weird Tales* Sep. 1927
(5) "The Gray People" by John Campbell Haywood (6500 words) from *The Witch's Tales* Nov. 1936
(6) "And Then No More" by Jay Tyler (4600 words)*
(4) "The Endocrine Monster" by R. Anthony (8500 words) from *Weird Tales* Apr. 1927
(1) "The Return of the Sorcerer" by Clark Ashton Smith (6750 words) from *Strange Tales* Sep. 1931
(3) "The Three from the Tomb" by Edmond Hamilton (13,250 words) from *Weird Tales* Feb. 1932

No. 9 Summer 1968 130 pgs 50¢

"The Black Mass" is illustrated by Amos Sewell. There's a strange half-page item called "The Death of Bolster" which is uncredited but appeared originally in the September 1931 issue of *Strange Tales*. The piece discusses the legend of a giant in Cornwall. There are "decorations" (RAWL's description) by artist Boyce on the final page of "The Last Archer." And one by Hugh Rankin on the last page of "Webbed Hands." "Webbed Hands" is illustrated by H.W. Wesso. "Hollywood Horror" is a Doctor Satan story. In "The Cauldron," RAWL addresses a letter writer's question about "framing a story in which a character is depicted as narrating the main story to some group or to a second 'first person' who writes it down," and defends the idea of a reprint magazine. It's interesting to note that, according to the advertisement on page 127, one could buy a "Life-Size Party Girl." Five foot four inches tall, with measurements of 36-22-36, all for only three bucks. Models included Joy and Candy. This seems a much more affordable solution to companionship than marriage, and I suspect many readers of the Health Knowledge zines took advantage of this offer.

SMS No. 9 Contents

(2) "The Black Mass" by Col. S. P. Meek (8250 words) from *Strange Tales* Nov.1931
(1) "The Last Archer" by Earl Peirce, Jr. (12,250 words) from *Weird Tales* Mar. 1937
(4) "The Sight of Roses" by Jay Tyler (7600 words)*
"Acrophobia" (verse) by L. Sprague de Camp
(5) "Webbed Hands" by Ferdinand Berthoud (8500 words) from *Strange Tales* Nov. 1931
(3) "Hollywood Horror" by Paul Ernst (12,750 words) from *Weird Tales* Oct. 1935

No. 10 Fall 1968 130 pgs 50¢

On "The Editor's Page," RAWL discusses the newly-issued *The Annotated Sherlock Holmes*, a massive, two-volume, 1452-page collection of Holmes stories. Joseph Doolin illustrates the Ward story. "The House Party at Smoky Island," which

Startling Mystery Stories No. 10 Fall 1968
Cover by Virgil Finlay

is illustrated by Vincent Napoli, sounds more like a Hardy Boys mystery than a featured story in *Weird Tales*. According to Lowndes' author notes, his "Settler's Wall" originally appeared in a shorter version as "The Long Wall" as by Wilfred Owen Morley. In the resurrected "Inquisitions" book review column, RAWL reviews *The Best From The Phantagraph*, edited by Donald A. Wollheim and the latest issues of fanzines *Lighthouse* (edited and published by Terry Carr) and *Habakkuk*. The Quinn story, a de Grandin, has story notes by RAWL. In them, he relates rumors about up to 200 unpublished de Grandin stories. Lowndes gets the story straight from the horse's mouth by writing to Quinn, who says "the correct figure of such unpublished manuscripts was no more or less than 0." RAWL goes on to explain that *Weird Tales* published every de Grandin Quinn sent them. "The Isle" is illustrated by an uncredited artist. In

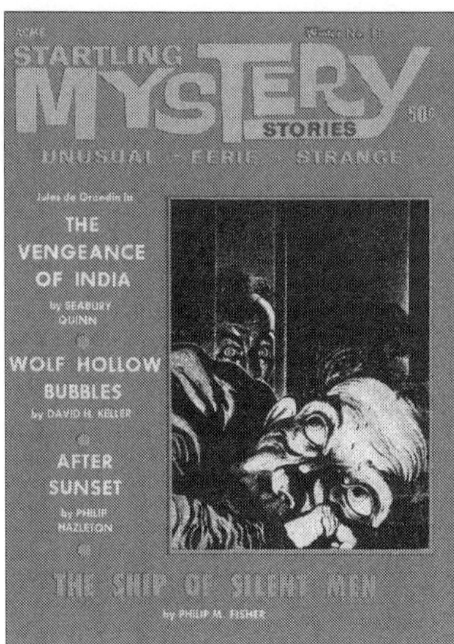

Startling Mystery Stories No. 11 Winter 1968/69
Cover by Virgil Finlay

"The Cauldron," RAWL announces the death of Anthony Boucher.

SMS No. 10 Contents

(3) "The House of the Living Dead"
by Harold Ward (13,750 words)
from *Weird Tales* Mar. 1932
(4) "The Indoor Safari" by Max Nugor
(2600 words)*
(5) "The House Party at Smoky Island"
by L. M. Montgomery (4000 words)
from *Weird Tales* Mar. 1935
(1) "Settler's Wall" by Robert A. W. Lowndes
(11,000 words) from *Stirring Science Stories* Mar. 1942
(2) "The Isle of Missing Ships"
by Seabury Quinn (17,500 words)
from *Weird Tales* Feb. 1926

No. 11 Winter 1968/69 130 pgs 50¢

On "The Editor's Page(s)," Lowndes discusses August Derleth's Solar Pons stories and their relation to Sherlock Holmes. "Wolf Hollow Bubbles," containing the popular Taine of San Francisco character created by Keller, originally appeared in a "slightly different" form in a pamphlet published in January 1934 by The ARRA Printers. The Howard story is illustrated (with a headlight shot!) by Hammond and "After Sunset" features an illo by Rafael de Soto. The Quinn story is a de Grandin. Rawl reviews *The Multi-Man* by Philip Harbottle and *The Necronomicon: A Study* by Mark Owings in "Inquisitions." He also notes the latest issues of *The Arkham Collector*, *Deeper Than You Think*, and *The Count Dracula Society Quarterly*. We also get the first mention of the first issue of Paul Ganley's long-running semi-pro fanzine, *Weirdbook*. The zine really hit the big time in 1984 when Ganley published "Gramma" by Stephen King in its 19th issue. Mike Ashley contributes to "The Cauldron."

SMS No. 11 Contents

(2) "Wolf Hollow Bubbles"
by David H. Keller, M.D. (8000 words)*
(t-5) "Mrs. Kaye" by Beverly Haaf (4000 words)*
(4) "The Haunter of the Ring"
by Robert E. Howard (7000 words)
from *Weird Tales* Jun 1934
(t-5) "The Vengeance of India"
by Seabury Quinn (7000 words)
from *Weird Tales* Apr. 1926
(1) "After Sunset" by Philip Hazleton (7500 words) from *Strange Tales* Nov. 1931
(3) "The Ship of Silent Men"
by Philip M. Fisher (16,500 words)
from *All-Story* Jan. 3, 1920
"The Whisperer" (Verse)
by Robert A. W. Lowndes

No. 12 Spring 1969 130 pgs 50¢

Issue No. 12 is the second most collectible Health Knowledge publication, not coincidentally because it features a very early story by Stephen King. Unlike the earlier "The Glass Floor," (*SMS* No. 6), "The Reaper's Image" can be found easily in King's 1986 collection, *Skeleton Crew*. In "The Editor's Page," RAWL discusses Edgar Al-

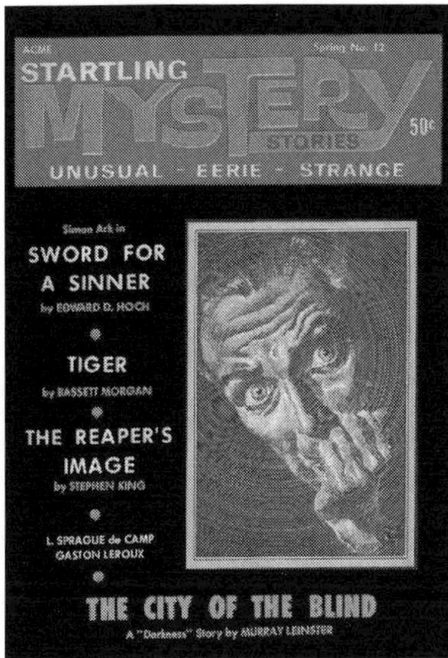

Startling Mystery Stories No. 12 Spring 1969
Cover by Virgil Finlay

Startling Mystery Stories No. 13 Summer 1969
Cover by Richard Schmand

lan Poe and his detective Auguste Dupin. Another (uncredited) small piece taken from the September 1931 issue of *Strange Tales* investigates "West England's Little Folk." "Inquisitions" features a review of *The Exploits of Chevalier Dupin* by Michael Harrison. The Hoch story features his ageless occult investigator, Simon Ark. Two letters from Mike Ashley in "The Cauldron." An Index to Volume 2 appears.

SMS No. 12 Contents

(t-3) "The Woman with the Velvet Collar" by Gaston Leroux (6500 words) from *Weird Tales* Oct. 1929

(t-3) "The Reaper's Image" by Stephen King (3250 words)*

"Sirrush" (verse) by L. Sprague de Camp

(2) "Sword for a Sinner" by Edward D. Hoch (13,500 words) from *The Saint Mystery Magazine* Oct. 1959

(t-3) "Tiger" by Bassett Morgan (7750 words) from *Strange Tales* Mar. 1932

(1) "The City of the Blind" by Murray Leinster (16,500 words) from *Argosy* Dec. 28, 1929

No. 13 Summer 1969 130 pgs 50¢

In "The Editor's Page," editor Robert A. W. Lowndes discusses Edgar Allan Poe's, "Murders in the Rue Morgue," and detective Auguste Dupin. J. Ramsey Campbell went on to be a big name in horror fiction, but by 1964 (at the age of 18) he'd already had a collection of his Cthulhu Mythos stories published by Arkham House, *The Inhabitant of the Lake and Other Less Welcome Tenants*. Campbell went on to write acclaimed novels such as *The Face That Must Die*, *The Doll Who Ate His Mother*, and *Incarnate*. He added "crime writer" to his resume with the excellent *The One Safe Place* in 1995. "Where There's Smoke" appears to be Welk's only published fiction (at least I find no other trace of her). RAWL mentions in Welk's bio that the author is awaiting the return of her Air Force Lieutenant husband from Pakistan. Perhaps that ended her career? "Ancient

Startling Mystery Stories No. 14 Winter 1970
Cover by Virgil Finlay

Startling Mystery Stories No. 15 Spring 1970
Cover by Robert Clewell

Fires" is followed by Part One of a chronological listing of the Jules de Grandin stories. Featured are four of the *Weird Tales* covers that highlighted a de Grandin story. There's also a bit of discussion of the cover and interior artists. As with Welk, I can find no further trace of Ken Porter after this appearance. In his "Inquisitions" column, RAWL reviews *Mr. Fairlee's Final Journey* by August Derleth and *The Sherlockian Doyle*, published by Luther Norris. RAWL also takes a look at three new fanzines: *The Baker Street Journal*, *The Armchair Detective*, and *The Rohmer Review*. Contributing to the letters page this issue is Stuart Schiff (editor and publisher of *Whispers*) and author David Drake.

SMS No. 13 Contents

(1) "The Gray Killer" by Everil Worrell (11,000 words) from *Weird Tales* Nov. 1929
(3) "The Scar" by J. Ramsey Campbell (7000 words)*
(6) "Where There's Smoke" by Donna Gould Welk (2200 words)*
(5) "Ancient Fires" by Seabury Quinn (16,500 words) from *Weird Tales* Sep. 1926
(4) "The Hansom Cab" by Ken Porter (3000 words)*
(2) "The Veil of Tanit" by Eugene de Rezske (9000 words) from *Strange Tales* Mar. 1932

No. 14 Winter 1969 130 pgs 50¢

In his "Editor's Page," RAWL discusses Philo Vance. "The Dogs" is illustrated by T. Wyatt Nelson. Dorothy Norman Cooke joins the League of Vanished Authors. Lupoff's contribution chronicles a fanciful visit between Edgar Rice Burroughs and Dr. Watson. "The Consuming Flame" is a Doctor Satan story. In "The Cauldron" (the letters page), RAWL discusses the Lancer paperback reprinting of *The Outsider*. Contributing letters are future monster movie TV host John Stanley (who asks after a new Robert Bloch hardcover, not knowing at the time that in a couple of decades he'd publish a Robert Bloch collection—*Lost in Time and Space with Lefty Feep*).

SMS No. 14 Contents

(2) "The Dogs of Doctor Dwann" by Edmond Hamilton (12,000 words) from *Weird Tales* Oct. 1932
(5) "The Parasite" by Dorothy Norman Cooke (6500 words)*
(1) "The Outsider" by H. P. Lovecraft (2750 words) from *Weird Tales* Apr. 1926
"The Crawler" (verse) by Robert A. W. Lowndes from *New Annals of Arkya*
(3) "The White Domino" by Urann Thayer (5750 words) from *Ghost Stories* Jul. 1928
"The Case of the Doctor Who Had No Business" by Richard Lupoff (4600 words)* (for some reason, this story was not rated in "The Reckoning")
(6) "The Feline Phantom" by Gilbert Draper (3750 words) from *Strange Tales* Mar. 1932
(4) "The Consuming Flame" by Paul Ernst (14,000 words) from *Weird Tales* Nov. 1935

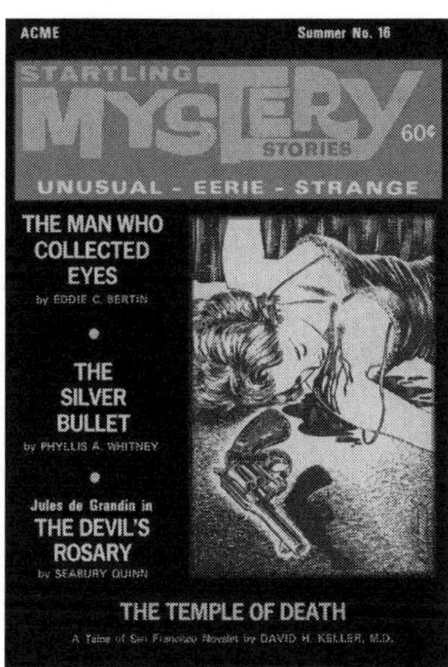

Startling Mystery Stories No. 16 Summer 1970
Cover by Richard Schmand

No. 15 Spring 1970 130 pgs 50¢

RAWL discusses Agatha Christie's sleuth Hercule Poirot in his "Editor's Page." "Horror Insured" is another tale in the saga of Doctor Satan (the final to be run by Health Knowledge). The story, it is noted, has been "slightly revised in order to eliminate certain inconsistencies in the original version." This was also done to "The Consuming Flame" in the previous issue. The Flagg story is illustrated by H.W. Wesso. "The Monkey's Paw" is illustrated by Maurice Greiffenhagen (since this illo is dated 1900, it's questionable as to whether this accompanied the story in its original appearance). Reviewed are *Who Done It?* by Ordean H. Hagen, a massive study of detective, mystery, and suspense fiction, and *A Compendium of Canonical Weaponry*, compiled by Bruce Dettman and Michael Bedford. Part Two of The Cases of Jules de Grandin, a chronological listing of the stories from 1933–1951, appears following "The Man Who Cast No Shadow." Four more Quinn *Weird Tales* covers are reproduced, and RAWL discusses the cover artists. Mike Ashley writes in.

SMS No. 15 Contents

(3) "Horror Insured" by Paul Ernst (14,500 words) from *Weird Tales* Jan. 1936
(4) "By Hands of the Dead" by Francis Flagg (6250 words) from *Strange Tales* Mar. 1932
(1) "The Monkey's Paw" by W. W. Jacobs (5500 words) from *Harper's* Sep. 1902
(5) "Cry, Baby, Cry" by Henry Slesar (4000 words)*
(2) "The Man Who Cast No Shadow" by Seabury Quinn (13,500 words) from *Weird Tales* Feb. 1927

No. 16 Summer 1970 130 pgs 60¢

RAWL discusses Miss Marple and various other topics in "The Editor's Page." The unfortunately titled "The Smell" is illustrated by H.W. Wesso. "The Temple of Death," a Taine of San Francisco tale, is a posthumous story, submitted by

Startling Mystery Stories No. 17 Fall 1970
Cover by Richard Schmand

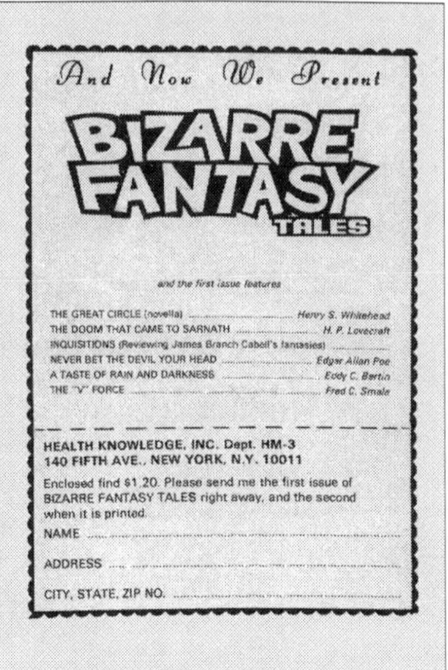

Startling Mystery Stories No. 17 Fall 1970
Back cover announcing *Bizarre Fantasy Tales*

Keller's widow. "The Silver Bullet" is illustrated by Vincent Napoli. "Inquisitions" features reviews of *Number Seven Queer Street* by Margery Lawrence and *The Science Fictional Sherlock Holmes*, an anthology of pastiches published by Abal Books. It's noted after "The Devil's Rosary" (a de Grandin story) that, as this issue went to press, RAWL had just received news of the passing of Seabury Quinn on December 24, 1969.

SMS No. 16 Contents

(5) "The Smell" by Francis Flagg (5000 words) from *Strange Tales* Jan. 1932
(3) "The Temple of Death" by David H. Keller, M. D. (12,000 words)*
(4) "The Silver Bullet" by Phyllis A. Whitney (8500 words) from *Weird Tales* Feb. 1935
(2) "The Man Who Collected Eyes" by Eddy C. Bertin (3100 words)*
(1) "The Devil's Rosary" by Seabury Quinn (18,500 words) from *Weird Tales* Apr. 1929

No. 17 Fall 1970 130 pgs 60¢

RAWL dissects G. K. Chesterton's sleuth, Father Brown in "The Editor's Page." An uncredited illo accompanies "The Infernal Shadow" (it looks to me like H.W. Wesso's work). T. Wyatt Nelson illustrates "The Vaults of Yoh-Vombis." "The Vicar of Hell" is the final Simon Ark story to be reprinted by Health Knowledge, which is unfortunate since I found the stories I read from the series to be top-notch pulpish fun. C. C. Senf, who did several sharp covers for *Weird Tales* in the early 1930s, illustrates the Jules de Grandin "The Bride of Dewer" (the last de Grandin to be reprinted by Lowndes). In his review of *A Compendium of Canonical Weaponry* (No. 15), Lowndes made a mistake about a revolver and fandom lets him know what they do in their spare time. Two full-holstered readers write in to rip RAWL a new one. The newest title, *Bizarre Fantasy Tales*, is featured in an ad on the back cover. Unfortunately, the zine would last only two issues.

SMS No. 17 Contents

"The Infernal Shadow" by Hugh B. Cave (10,500 words) from *Strange Tales* Oct. 1932

"The Vaults of Yoh-Vombis" by Clark Ashton Smith (8750 words) from *Weird Tales* May 1932

"Laura" by Joseph H. Bloom (4250 words)*

"The Vicar of Hell" by Edward D. Hoch (10,500 words) from *Famous Detective* Aug. 1956

"The Bride of Dewer" by Seabury Quinn (13,500 words) from *Weird Tales* Jul. 1930

No. 18 March 1971 130 pgs 75¢

The final issue of *SMS* is the only one to be tagged with a month rather than a season. RAWL discusses Nero Wolfe in his "Editor's Page." RAWL reviews *The Secrets of Dr. Taverner* by Dion Fortune, the latest issue of *The Rohmer Review*, and a chapbook by Jacob C. Solovay, *Sherlock Holmes: Two Sonnet Sequences*. An uncredited illo accompanies "The Golden Patio." F. Paul Wilson went on to become the best-selling author of *The Keep* and several novels featuring hit-man Repairman Jack. "The Storm That Had to Be Stopped" is a follow-up to "The Darkness on Fifth Avenue" (*SMS* No. 5) and "The City of the Blind" (*SMS* No. 12). The final "Cauldron" is given a nice illustration (uncredited) and features a letter from Richard Lupoff (concerning his story in No. 14). RAWL notes in answer to a reader's query that the remainder of Doctor Satan stories will be reprinted in good time. Another NRA member/*SMS* subscriber writes in to give RAWL a piece of his mind. As noted, this was the final issue of *SMS*. However, a "Next Issue" ad featured with a snippet from "The Full-Moon Maniac," an original story written by David Charles Paskow, a frequent letter writer to the Health Knowledge digests. It's doubtful this story was ever published (at least not in a professional magazine).

Startling Mystery Stories No. 18 March 1971
Cover uncredited

SMS No. 18 Contents

"Drome of the Living Dead" by John Scott Douglas (11,000 words) from *Weird Tales* Aug. 1935

"Conjured" by Larry Eugene Meredith (2300 words)*

"The Golden Patio" by Aubrey Feist (6000 words) from *Strange Tales* Jun. 1932

"The Cleaning Machine" by F. Paul Wilson (2000 words)*

"The Storm That Had To Be Stopped" by Murray Leinster (27,000 words) from *Argosy* Mar. 1, 1930

Peter Enfantino continues to write about various horror and war comic books on <barebonesez.blogspot.com> twice weekly, covering the Warren Publishing books, Atlas /Marvel pre-code horror books, and DC's war comics.

Kromaflies

Fantasy fiction by Joe Wehrle, Jr.
Art by Carolyn Cosgriff

"The kromaflies are coming!"

"The kromaflies!"

Raven of Narbek ran past the excited, chanting crowd of children assembled in the clearing and made for the leuritan of her uncle. The daybirds and aragats shrieked mimicry of the voices below, punctuating the shouts of the young Narbekians, as Raven's soft yefskin boots scuffed through the acridly fragrant grasses which cushioned the Narbek Forest.

She could well remember joining in the childish excitement, but those days were past, for she was grown and now would watch with the quiet wonder of an elder. Or so she told herself.

Brimming with glad visions of other kromafly swarmings, Raven was oblivious of her own movements as she mounted the carved stairs within Boar's tree-dwelling. When the spiraling steps ended abruptly, the girl put her head out through an orifice in the great trunk and, shoving flaxen leuritan leaves aside, scanned the heavens. From her high vantage point, she at last spied the dark, slowly-moving cloud drifting from the Blackened Mountains and spreading above the vast floor of leuritan trees.

Raven withdrew from the window as the sound of heavier boots signaled the ascent of her uncle.

"Coming, are they?" Boar asked, peering out at the sky.

"The first in a long time!"

"Well, we've had no excitement around here," the old man rumbled. "I welcome them." He settled his stout frame onto a fur-draped bench which protruded from the wall.

"How do they do it?"

"How? A better question might be 'why?' After the End of the Old and the Beginning of the New, a lot of things were changed, many for the worse. The kromaflies changed for the better. They help us rediscover some of the good old things that were lost."

"Why can't we rediscover them ourselves?"

"We *can* think up new tools, and find ways to fix some of the old weapons," Boar told her, "but the things the kromaflies give us are the pictures and ideas that can be created just once, and never again. You remember the last one, don't you? Stag, your father, has it in the counciltree."

"I used to help prepare the food there," Raven confided, "so that I might gaze at something from the lost past."

A murmur of voices rose higher and higher from the clearing outside. The air seemed to squirm and ripple as the kromaflies, indistinguishable as tiny grains of sand, constantly changed hues, tumbling into one another and filling the forest glades with their humming. Raven blinked, amazed as always.

Four men under Stag's direction were stretching a screen of finely-woven fibers between the trees. An ancient crone carefully brushed a sticky mixture of herb juices over the taut surface.

The kromaflies hovered before the screen, shifting and mingling, mingling and shifting. As the mass stabilized, a hush fell over the assembled foresters.

A stone wall, thin as a leaf, stood before them, the same stone wall upon which the kromaflies en mass had come to rest one spring morning, camouflaging themselves with all the hues of the wall, remembering the formation throughout their short existence, and duplicating it now that this existence was nearly at an end.

With a long brushlike implement, Stag dissipated the wall before the insects could attach themselves to the sticky screen. The mass reformed, stubbornly.

Now the ragged side of a cliff faced the watchers, flattened grotesquely to only two dimensions. Again the brush scattered the altering insects.

Time after time the kromaflies formed, reformed, changed colors. Time after time the brush did its work.

At last, a murmur from the audience. Lines were forming, a diagram of some lost device was taking shape before the screen. Stag lowered the brush, staring anxiously at the formation.

Discovered in some burned and buried city or in some deep and forgotten cavern, it was reproduced exactly as found, the closely-packed bodies of the kromaflies duplicating both seared edge and dog-eared corner.

The diagram represented what appeared to be a great machine, shown with all its integral parts. To Raven, standing slightly apart from the assembly, some of the components looked vaguely similar to those in the few existing energy devices which the foresters used for carving out their tree homes or baking their breads, but this was obviously in far larger scale.

She felt a surge of excitement when she recognized many of the parts shown. Foraging parties frequently brought back metal parts from the ruined cities. Larger devices which were found to hold the forgotten power sources were buried, though, as they could not safely be taken apart or used to make tools.

Surely something like this could be built from scavenged pieces without too much difficulty. Raven wondered what possible purpose it could have. Then she thought she knew, and she was afraid.

Stag continued to watch the kromafly formation uncertainly. Raven ran to the center of the clearing, stopping short when Stag turned toward her. He looked from the young girl's anguished face to the duplicated plan before him. It was apparent that he, too, knew what the object could be.

The formation was beginning its slow drift to the sticky surface. Stag gripped the long brush handle tightly, biting his lip. Suddenly he swept the brush through the kromaflies with one violent motion.

When the insects reformed again, there were exclamations of awe and appreciation. A city stood, white towers gleaming, against an evening sky. The bodies of the kromaflies formed the artist's very brushstrokes, reproduced his most subtle shades. A lost painting by a forgotten master.

Undisturbed, the kromaflies sank to the stretched surface, laid their eggs in the sticky coating and expired. When the new insects hatched, they would leave behind them on the painting a fluid which would so harden that only the sharpest knife could cut through it.

Glad of any excuse for celebration, the foresters lingered in the clearing. Tables were brought and food and drink laid out. Small groups gravitated toward the stretched screen to get a first-hand look, while Stag and the other community leaders discussed plans for the storage and eventual disposition of the precious artifact.

At last Raven watched her father separate himself from the others and disappear into the family's leuritan. She gave him a few minutes, then she followed into the great tree, for she had things to say and things to ask.

Shadows moved in the chamber to the right, so she didn't mount the internal staircase, but quietly moved toward where she thought Stag must be working. He had a large sheet of barkpaper spread upon the tree-carved table, and he was furiously outlining shapes on it with a thin marking stick. It only took Raven a second to see what he was drawing.

"Father!"

Stag looked up and frowned at Raven's expression.

"I know. I know"

"But . . . why?"

"Because it's knowledge. *Dangerous* knowledge, to be sure. Dangerous knowledge that our family will have to caretake until the energy this machine harnesses may be turned to peaceful pursuits, and that's a serious responsibility. But I can't see knowledge destroyed when even the *barest* chance exists of it being used for good.

Raven took a breath. "I hope you're right."

Stag nodded and slowly laid a hand on her shoulder. "I may have just staked our lives on it."

Joe Wehrle, Jr. (1941–2017) was an illustrator, cartoonist, writer and musician. His work appeared in *Galaxy*, *If*, *The Menomonee Falls Gazette*, *Vampirella*, *Two-Gun Raconteur*, and numerous other publications. His stories continue to appear in *The Digest Enthusiast* courtesy of Jillian Rouse.

Carolyn Cosgriff is an artist and designer. Her prints, calendars, and sculptures are available online at <HissBuzzHum.com>

Alfred Hitchcock Mystery Magazine May/June 2019

Review by Richard Krauss
Art by Brian Buniak

"There were thirteen of them all right, though the last one was holed up in a coffin."
"The Case of the Thirteenth Beard" by Joe Helgerson *AHMM* May/June 2019

Linda Landrigan opens the issue with "Called to Crime," a brief introduction that leads to "The Lineup," short bios of the issue's writers. Then, it's on to the stories:

Bonus Round by Joseph S. Walker

As a data analyst for NYPD, the first person narrator of this police procedural, is in an ideal position to observe Detective Karen Byers' investigation of the murder of twenty-two-year-old Jessica Osman, undetected. He's a trivia buff and intersperses the story with trivial nuggets, which provide strange—yet successful—breaks throughout the narrative. Osman competed in the trivia contests popular in NYC's neighborhood bars. In fact, she played along in one the night she was murdered. The circumstantial evidence against Byers' key suspect comes fast and easy, but was he set up or hideously guilty?

Finite Jest by Chris Muessig, art by Noah Bailey

The mystery of the jester at times feels almost like background in this chronicle of PFC Jake Miller and his fellow soldiers as they make their way from train to ship toward action in Europe during the great war. At sea, the constant threat of U-boats adds a layer of suspense to the story, but the detailed account of the main characters' lives and feelings during their journey overshadows even the spare moments of action. This one's a treat for those who revel in the immersion of history, location, and atmosphere.

Private Justice by Steven Gore

Fiction gives readers a view of

the world from a new perspective. Sometimes it's simpler than reality, painted in black and white, with only two choices: right or wrong. Other times it reveals the grey areas of every choice—even murder, as in this story about an ex-professor, his wife, and his former students. Gore delivers a brilliant mystery story demonstrating the nuances of motivation that drive his characters' actions. The title reflects the private justice of closed communities like universities as well as an individual's personal viewpoint.

Real Cowgirls Don't Cry
by Catherine Dilts

Someone's planted a crop of marijuana in the rickety old shed on Katie Roberts' ranch. The nail board booby-traps around it are meant to ward off intruders, but when a favorite mare punctures a hoof on one, the Rocking R is soon swarming with attention. Katie is surrounded by plenty of suspects, each with engaging quirks and foibles.

Buck and Wiley Make Their Own Luck by Parker Littlewood, art by Hank Blaustein

Next, we move from ranch to trail, but with a unique perspective—our first-person narrator is a horse. Buck steals the show by a nose as his loquacious pardner, Wiley, talks his way around one ambush after another. Great fun!

Flamingo Bingo
by Terrie Farley Moran

The senior scene at the Sunshine Palms condos is a bit of an eye-opener for Renee Saperstein when she visits the sunshine state to celebrate her mom's birthday. Bike

rides, pickleball, yoga, and bingo—the seemingly constant churn of activity is exhausting for the "youngster." And so is the mix of all those senior personalities. Like Henry, on the make for any woman—married or otherwise. ". . . we're old 'uns but not dead 'uns." a resident advises her. The scramble of temperaments and agendas soon collide when old Henry's number comes up.

Bonded by Mark Joslyn

Poor Roosevelt, coerced into posting bond for his sister's serial abuser, he feels nearly as trapped by circumstances as his sibling. To make matters worse, the perp shows no sign of remorse. In fact, he's clueless. But Roosevelt is tired of how this story ends and decides it's time for a rewrite.

The Case of the Thirteenth Beard (Sheriff Huck Finn) by Joe Helgerson

The first Sherriff Huck Finn story appeared in *AHMM* June 2002, making this adventure the Marquis, Iowa lawman's seventh appearance. I don't know about its predecessors, but this one is narrated by his deputy, Joe, and full of humorously quirky characters and circumstances. When the Circle of the Beard rides into town—twelve men upright, one prone—the sheriff is suspicious the death of the Thirteenth Beard wasn't the accident the twelve describe. The story is long enough to include several other kooky secrets and mysteries, and Helgerson does a good job of weaving them all together by its disarming end.

Photo Finished by Melissa Fall

There's nothing like a murder to bring folks together. Before Kathy discovers her neighbor's body in the parking lot of her apartment building, her life is a wreck. But slowly, as she and the cops piece things together, the mystery and her future begin to resolve. An issue highlight.

Thick as Thieves by Gigi Vernon, art by Maggie Ivy

Honor among thieves is only veneer in this noirish tale of pickpockets and robbers, set in folly olde England. Once a victim, newly widowed Pamela joins Betty and Ned, who are happy to sponsor her apprenticeship in crime. But the new triangular partnership soon turns dour and implodes. Another strong entry for the issue.

A Work in Progress by Elizabeth Zelvin

If you see something and don't say something, is it a crime? Jack dumps Hester for a younger woman, and they all end up at a writing workshop. It's easy to see Hester's life reflected in her WIP. "I'd taken notes on how I felt about Jack's arrival, every shifting nuance. Marjorie wasn't me, and Hank wasn't Jack, exactly, but the more I understood Hester and Jack, the more lifelike I'd be able to make Marjorie and Hank."

The final confrontation between wife and husband at a deserted beach is a bittersweet mix of raging emotions—love, play, anger, and violence that even the Atlantic Ocean can't sweep away.

Blind Spot by Mark Thielman

An evening ride-along courtesy of veteran police officer Tim Johnson in Charlie District, "a community of people who never knew their minds with any clarity. They lived lives of indecision and indifference, smoking and drinking, eating and sleeping, the neighborhood existed with a collective shrug and what-the-hell surprise." A pull-over for failure to signal is just an excuse to ensure a known drug dealer, fresh out of the can, heads home and stays out of trouble—at least for the night. "Officer Johnson always saw his job more as doing justice rather than enforcing the law."

Later, a second traffic violation leads to a medicated, potentially suicidal woman packing heat in her purse. He secures her promise not to harm herself. "Get yourself home and stay there. Tomorrow, first thing, call your psychiatrist. Tell your doc about tonight."

While approaching a vehicle he's pulled over; Johnson is careful to use the blind spot to remain invisible to the driver as long as possible. Unfortunately, sometimes good people like Johnson have blind spots of their own.

The Thief (A Mystery Classic)
by Anna Katharine Green

Editor Linda Landrigan introduces the story by Green (1846–1945) who wrote thirteen novels featuring detective Ebenezer Gryce, influencing "such later masters of the craft as Agatha Christie and Arthur Conan Doyle."

Perhaps "theft" is too strong a word for the polite company attending wealthy Mr. Sedwick's well-attended dinner party when a rare and valuable coin goes missing—and perhaps not. The hunt/investigate in its wake is remarkably civilized and yields unexpected results—including a foil.

Puzzles, Contests, and More

More than any other digest in the Penny Publications lineup, *AHMM* takes advantage of the company's vast resources in puzzles. Mark Lagasse's anagram, Arlene Fisher's acrostic, and the Mysterious Photograph $25 fiction contest appear in every issue. The winner of the contest, from two issues back, is presented in "The Story That Won," in 250 words or less. This time it's "After the Party's Over" by Charlotte Stacey, about a New Year's Eve brawl and its aftermath.

Finally, the review column "Booked and Printed" is ably tackled by Laurel Flores Fantauzzo, who examines *Sugar Run* by Mesha Maren and *An Elderly Lady is Up to No Good* by Helene Tursten.

Wrap-Up

The crimes in *AHMM*'s stories range from everyday mundane to gut-wrenching murder, driven by perfectly reasonable or unfathomable desires. Readers are always privy to the solution of its mysteries, but justice may or may not involve the law.

The Master of Suspense's sardonic humor is clearly evident in several adventures, while others are more deadly serious. It's characters that steal the show in *AHMM*. How they process what the world does to them, and what they do to themselves, shapes their narratives and their frequently faulty results.

Alfred Hitchcock Mystery Magazine
Vol. 64 No. 5 & 6 May/June 2019
Publisher: Peter Kanter
Editor: Linda Landrigan
Associate Editor: Jackie Sherbow
Senior Director of Art & Production: Porter C. McKinnon
Senior AD: Victoria Green
Cover: Shutterstock, design by Vicki Green
192 pages, $7.99
<alfredhitchcockmysterymagazine.com>

How Sol Cohen "Saved" Amazing Stories

Article by Vince Nowell, Sr.

A brief review of Sol Cohen's Ultimate Publishing and Distribution (UPD) operations and the "Ultimate" digest reprints.

The Situation

In May 1965 an energetic former Avon Publications editor named Sol Cohen, who had guided the Galaxy Group magazines for several years, formed his own firm, Ultimate Publishing and Distribution (UPD). He then (August) purchased the digest magazines *Amazing Stories Fact & Fiction* and its companion, *Fantastic Stories of Imagination*, from publisher Ziff Davis. Cohen retitled them as simply *Amazing Stories* (thus restoring the original historic title) and *Fantastic Stories* (evolved from editor Howard Browne's very classy early 1950s *Fantastic*).

Cohen impacted the science fiction and fantasy (SFF) genre by using the acquired story rights to Ziff Davis' owned material from *Amazing Stories* (dating back to 1926), the pulp *Fantastic Adventures*, and the digest *Fantastic*. By reprinting such material, Cohen produced *eleven different digest-sized reprint magazines under 17 different titles* from 1965–1975. That adds up to a total of 115 issues of reprints!

The catch was that Cohen paid no royalties for reprinting the older stories. Thus, with the monetary success of these reprint titles it was possible for Cohen to continue to publish the ailing *Amazing Stories* and *Fantastic* magazines, both of which carried a lot of new tales—for which the authors were —indeed—paid.

GIANT 35th ANNIVERSARY ISSUE 196 pages
Amazing
Fact and Science Fiction
stories
APRIL
50¢
7 OF THE GREATEST SF STORIES EVER WRITTEN
I, ROCKET
by Ray Bradbury
DEVOLUTION
by Edmond Hamilton
ARMAGEDDON—2419
(The First Buck Rogers Story)
by Philip Francis Nowlan
JOHN CARTER AND THE GIANT OF MARS
by Edgar Rice Burroughs
OUT OF THE SUB-UNIVERSE
by R. F. Starzl
THE FLYING FOOL
by David H. Keller, M.D.
I, ROBOT by Eando Binder
Special Article by HUGO GERNSBACK
Founder of AMAZING

This composite front cover for *Amazing Stories* April 1961, the 35th anniversary of the magazine. It featured reprinted front cover artwork by Frank R. Paul and some classic anniversary reprint stories, all under the editorial guidance of Cele Goldsmith.

The *Amazing Fantastic* Account!

Amazing Stories was the pioneer all-science-fiction magazine founded by electrical-hobbiest Hugo Gernsback in 1926. It was yanked away from Gernsback by a rival publisher in 1929. Nearly ten years later it was purchased by Ziff Davis Publications (1938).

Fantastic, a digest-sized fantasy magazine, was published from 1952 to 1980. It was founded under Ziff Davis as a second companion to *Amazing Stories*. Early sales were

Amazing Stories Feb. 1966 under editor Joseph Ross. Cover by Frank R. Paul (reprint)

good, and Ziff Davis quickly decided to switch *Amazing* from pulp format to digest, and to merge their other science fiction pulp, *Fantastic Adventures* into the digest *Fantastic.*

But within a few years sales fell, and editor Howard Browne was forced to switch the focus of *Fantastic* to science fiction rather than fantasy. Browne, who did not like science fiction, lost interest in the magazine as a result. *Fantastic* continued under Browne, and then his successor, Paul W. Fairman, who had left *IF* (Quinn Publishing), and joined Ziff Davis in September 1952. He became the Managing Editor by the middle of 1953. A stream of editors then followed, as related below.

An identity crisis developed in time, and *Fantastic*'s title began a series of changes. It became *Fantastic Science Fiction.* Even its digest companion was affected when, in March 1958, *Amazing Stories* became *Amazing Science Fiction Stories* in an attempt to remain "current" with the variable trends in SFF.

Then Ziff Davis switched to *Fantastic Science Fiction Stories* but later retitled it again to *Fantastic Stories of Imagination.* This was the same month that witnessed the new title *Amazing Stories—Fact & Science Fiction.*

A Tale of Many Editors

The list below identifies *Amazing Stories* and *Fantastic*'s acting editors after Raymond A. Palmer, who held the post from 1938 to 1949. Palmer stepped down to found his own publishing company.

- Howard Browne (Succeeded Ray Palmer after 1949–Aug. 1956)
- Paul Fairman (Oct. 1956–Nov. 1958)
- Cele Goldsmith (Dec. 1958–June 1965; married name, Cele G. Lalli from 7/64)
- [Sol Cohen buys out Ziff Davis in May 1965]
- Joseph Ross (Sep. 1965–Nov. 1967) (Real name: Joseph Wroz)
- Harry Harrison (Jan. 1968–Oct. 1968)
- Barry N. Malzberg (Dec. 1968–Apri.1969)
- Ted White (June 1969–Jan. 1979)
- Elinor Mavor (Apr. 1979–Oct. 1980; stayed with *Amazing* until at least May 1981)

Cele Goldsmith

In November 1955, Ziff Davis hired an assistant, Cele Goldsmith, who began by helping with two new magazines under development, *Dream World* and *Pen Pals.* She also read the slush piles for all the magazines. Then she was given more responsibility when in 1957 she was made managing editor of both *Amazing* and *Fantastic.* By the end of 1958, she became editor, replacing Fairman, who left to edit *Ellery Queen's Mystery Magazine* (Mercury Publications). Cele Goldsmith (who became Cele Lalli via marriage in 1964) stayed on as editor for seven years.

She brought a number of new SF writers aboard and helped stoke their careers. She spanned the transition from what I still call "Golden Age" SF to the new stuff of the 1960s and later. She helped to invigorate the nascent sword and sorcery subgenre. During the early 1960s Goldsmith managed to make *Fantastic* and *Amazing*, in the words of SF magazine historian Mike Ashley, "the [two] best-looking and brightest" magazines around. This applied both to the magazines' contents as well as to front covers, where Goldsmith used artists such as Alex Schomburg (born Alejandro Schomburg y Rosa in May 1905; died April 1998) and Leo Summers.

Amazing Stories April 1967 under editor Joseph Ross. Cover by Frank R. Paul (reprint)

Enter Sol Cohen [Hiss!! Boo!!]

When in May 1965 Sol Cohen formed Ultimate Publishing and Distribution (UPD) and acquired the Ziff Davis SFF mags, Cohen incurred the wrath of the newly formed Science Fiction Writers of America (SFWA). According to SF historian Robert Holdstock (*Encyclopedia of Science Fiction*, London 1978), Cohen did not pay royalties to the authors of the stories he reprinted. For ten years he published a series of cheap-looking, non-interior-illustrated "plain-jane" digest-sized magazines that even collectors disdained at the time, per Mike Resnick in his magazine price guide, *Guide to the Fantastics*, 1976.

Cohen had decided to make his magazines as profitable as possible by filling them only with reprints. This was possible because Ziff Davis had acquired second serial rights—technically, therefore, all rights—for all the stories they had published. Since Cohen had bought the back-file of stories, he was able to reprint virtually everything using these rights without paying the authors for republishing their stories.

Yes, it's legal under U.S. copyright laws, although it isn't considered good practice. Authors are advised to sell only their "First North American Serial Rights" when submitting material to publishers. Even that can backfire, as happened to me when a magazine article I sold to an education journal later appeared in a compendium textbook on the topic of reading, with no payment (nor even notification). At least I received writing credit in the textbook.

When the publisher change came, Cele (Goldsmith) Lalli decided that she did not want to work for Cohen, and stayed with Ziff Davis. Her last issue was June 1965. Cohen replaced her with Joseph Wrzos, who used the name "Joseph Ross" on the magazines.

Amazing Stories Sep. 1969 under editor Ted White. Cover by Johnny Bruck

Cohen had met Wrzos at the *Galaxy* offices not long before. Wrzos was teaching English full-time but had worked for Gnome Press as an assistant editor in 1953–1954.

By using a reprint-only policy, Cohen saved about $8,000 a year between the two magazines. (That seems so little nowadays.) While this was financially successful, it created conflict for Cohen, as noted above. Harry Harrison, an established SF author, had been involved in negotiations between SFWA and Cohen. When an agreement was reached in 1967, Cohen asked Harrison if he would take over as editor of both magazines.

Harry Harrison and Barry Malzberg

Cohen agreed to phase out the reprints by the end of 1967, and Harrison took the editorial job, but the reprints in *Fantastic* and *Amazing* continued, and Harrison decided to quit in February 1968. He recommended Barry Malzberg as his replacement. Cohen had worked with Malzberg at the Scott Meredith Literary Agency and felt Malzberg would be more cooperative than Harrison. Malzberg, however, turned out to be just as unwilling as Harrison to work with Cohen if the unpaid reprints continued, and soon regretted taking the job.

In October 1968 Cohen refused to pay for a cover that Malzberg had commissioned. Malzberg insisted, threatening to resign if Cohen did not agree. Cohen contacted Robert Silverberg, then the president of SFWA, and told him (falsely) that Malzberg had actually resigned. Silverberg recommended Ted White as a replacement. Cohen secured White's agreement and then fired Malzberg. White took over in October 1968, but because there was a backlog of stories that Malzberg had acquired, the first issue on which White was credited as editor was the June 1969 issue.

Ted White

Like his immediate predecessors, White took the job on condition that the reprints would be phased out. It was some time before this was achieved: there was at least one reprinted story in every issue until the end of 1971. The February 1972 issue contained some artwork reprinted from 1939 and later. *Fantastic*'s circulation was about 37,000 when White took over; only about 4 percent of this was subscription sales. Cohen's wife filled the subscriptions from their garage, and according to White, Cohen regarded this as a burden, and never tried to increase the subscription base. Despite White's efforts, *Fantastic*'s circulation fell to less than 24,000 in the summer of 1975. *Amazing* was doing a bit better.

Ted White was working at a low salary, with unpaid help from friends to read unsolicited submissions—at one point he even introduced a 25¢ reading fee for manuscripts from unpublished writers; the fee would be refunded if White bought the story. White sometimes found himself at odds with Cohen's business partner, Arthur Bernhard, due to their different political views. White's unhappiness with his working conditions culminated in his resignation after Cohen refused his proposal to publish *Fantastic* as a slick magazine, with larger pages and higher quality paper. White commented in an article in *Science Fiction Review* that he had brought to the magazines:

> "*. . . a lot of energy and enthusiasm and a great many ideas for their [the magazines'] improvement . . . Well, I have put into effect nearly every idea which I was allowed to follow through on . . . and have spent most of my energy and enthusiasm.*"

Nevertheless, White was unable to halt the slide in circulation completely. It even rose a little in 1977. That year Cohen lost $15,000 on the magazines and decided to sell. He spent some time looking for a new publisher—editor Roy Torgeson was one of those interested—but on September 15, 1978, he sold his half of the business to Arthur Bernhard, his partner.

White renewed his suggestions for improving the formats of the magazines: he wanted to make *Fantastic* the same size as *Time* and believed he could avoid the mistakes that had been made by other SF magazines that had tried that approach.

White also proposed an increase in the budget and asked for a raise. Bernhard not only turned down White's ideas but also stopped paying him. White responded by resigning. His last official day as editor was November 9, 1978; the last issues under his control were in January 1979. He returned all submissions to their authors, saying that he had been told to do so by Bernhard, who in turn denied that.

James Gunn, in his SF history, says Ted White was very capable and "probably *Amazing Stories*' best editor ever." White had worked hard to make the magazine successful, introducing artwork from artists who had made their names in comics, and working with new authors such as Gordon Eklund. His budget for fiction was low, but he was occasionally able to find good stories, from well-known writers, which had been rejected by other markets.

When he stepped down, White had been editor for nearly ten years. He was replaced by Elinor Mavor. Within two years Bernhard decided to close down *Fantastic*, by "merging" it with *Amazing*, which had always had slightly higher circulation.

The Ultimate Reprints

In his *The Encyclopedia of Science Fiction* (1978) Robert Holdstock wrote that from 1965–1972 [sic, he meant 1975] "Cohen instituted a policy of almost total reprint, including a number of all-reprint magazines like *Thrilling Science Fiction* and *Science Fiction Clas-*

sics." The reprint magazines made sufficient money to subsidize *Amazing* and *Fantastic*'s reversion to publishing new fiction, "but since the last reprint folded in 1975, that support has not been there." Holdstock later asks rhetorically if *Fantastic* is still alive, and predicts *Amazing*'s imminent demise as its circulation declines.

Mike Resnick, in his buyer's guide, explains that Sol Cohen's publications were reprints of *Amazing Stories*, *Fantastic Adventures*, *Fantastic* and even reaching back to the 1930s with *Wonder Stories*, and other material from the Gernsback—Tech Publications era. Most of Ultimate's reprints from the mid-1960s to the early 1970s, Resnick noted, were worth at best 50¢ apiece. [Revised to 1995 values: about $1.35 each.] By the 2010s and after they were reselling for $3 to $6 each.

While this remarkable run of publishing not only upset many SF writers, I am sure more than one publisher on either side of the Atlantic was aggravated by the apparent pirating of other SFF magazines' titles. These mags are a great source for reprint stories from magazines that are growing evermore scarce and/or expensive for readers to acquire. [The same is true for *Famous Fantastic Mysteries*.]

Because these mags have been held in such low esteem in the decades following their publication I suspect many of them got trashed. But scarcity breeds value in the collecting field. So, the Ultimate reprints, with some still available at reasonable prices from dealers, could well be "sleepers" for collectors.

UPD Magazines

Following are the UPD magazine titles, listed in the general order of founding, and showing the title changes that occurred. Space does not permit a detailed listing of reprinted contents.

Great Science Fiction Magazine Winter 1965 (January 1966)–Spring 1971 (21 issues). Became *Science Fiction Greats* Winter 1969–Spring 1970; then became *SF Greats* Spring 1970–Spring 1971.

The Most Thrilling Science Fiction Ever Told Summer (June) 1966–July 1975 (42 issues). Became *Thrilling Science Fiction* Spring 1975–July 1975 (but had absorbed *Science Fiction Adventure Classics* in November 1974).

Science Fiction Classics Summer (June) 1967–November 1974 (30 issues). Became *Science Fiction Adventure Classics* Winter 1969–November 1974, when it was then absorbed by *Thrilling Science Fiction* (above).

Strange Fantasy Spring 1969–Fall 1970 (6 issues).

Science Fiction Adventures Yearbook January 1970 (1 issue).

Space Adventures (Classics) Winter (January) 1970–Summer 1971 (6 issues).

Fantastic Adventures Yearbook Spring (February) 1970 (1 issue).

Science Fiction Classics Annual March 1970 (1 issue).

Astounding Stories Yearbook Summer (May) 1970–Fall 1970 (2 issues), but second issue retitled *Astounding SF* (Fall 1970).

Science Fantasy Yearbook Summer (June) 1970–Spring 1971 (4 issues), but after its first issue became *Science Fantasy* Fall 1970–Spring 1971.

The Strangest Stories Ever Told Summer (June) 1970 (1 issue).

Weird Mystery Fall 1970–Summer 1971 (4 issues). Reprints from *Weird Tales* and similar (probably material in public domain).

Sword & Sorcery Annual Winter/Spring 1975 (1 issue). One story from *Weird Tales*, the remainder are from issues of *Fantastic* in the 1960s.

Wrapping Up the Amazing Stories Story

Under Ultimate (UPD) the mag managed to achieve a 55th-anniversary issue (May 1981). As of March 1985 *Amazing Science Fiction Stories* (a renewed title variation), combined with *Fantastic Stories*, was now being published by Dragon Publications (TSR) of Lake Geneva, Wisconsin. It was under the editorship of George H. Scithers.

Ironically, also by the decade of the 1980s, Steven Spielberg began airing his television stories under the series title *Amazing Stories*. These episodes were moderately successful for about two seasons.

At the end of 1994, the magazine was still being published—once again as just *Amazing Stories*. However, the magazine died with the Winter 1995 issue, only to be revived again briefly in Summer 1998. The last publisher of *Amazing* as a paperbound mag that I know of was Wizards of the Coast, a gaming company from Japan. They brought it back as a slick quarterly, hiring Kim Mohan as editor, the same post he had held under TSR after Scithers.

Some of the driving forces behind the magazine were John Gregory Betancourt, Orson Scott Card, Ben Bova (formerly editor of *Analog*), the late James Tiptree, Jr. (Alice Sheldon), again the late Ursula K. LeGuin, and author Robert Silverberg.

This revival was documented in my fanzine, *The Eclectic Collector—Book Three* in an article by Ted White. White e-mailed me in May 1998 to say this regarding the Wizards take-over from TSR:

> *"I hear there will be gaming tie-ins, maybe gaming oriented fiction. In its last [previous] incarnation AMAZING published 'previews' and tease-chapters from forthcoming books. along with full-color book cover art, as promotional tie-ins with advertisers—an editorially dubious practice. I wouldn't be surprised if this idea is extended into gaming this time around."*

That revival only ran for ten issues and was, to me, unremarkable. And so ended the saga of Hugo Gernsback's pioneer American science fiction magazine. Started in 1926, it met its destiny in 2000—that's a respectable 74 or so years.

I have read that *Amazing* later lived on in online digital format (and perhaps POD). I have also read that a newer revival is in the works and is now up and thriving (?), so that *Amazing Stories* may even see the light of day as a century-old publication. Also, what I could find online was a bit about a TV revival. The applicable *Amazing* cliché is: Time will tell.

Vince Nowell (Sr.), a sixth-generation native Californian, is a retired technical writer. As the editor of the Operating Manual for the J-2 rocket engine, he was on the project team for the Apollo 11 Moon Landing Program in 1969. His aerospace background encompasses missile instrumentation and test engineering. An avid reader since elementary school, Vince has been reading and collecting science fiction & fantasy since 1950. With a degree in history, a subject he taught in community colleges, he now enjoys researching the history of SF magazines and the backgrounds of authors.

Charlie Chan Mystery Magazine

Article by Richard Krauss

"Now in a series especially written, entirely brand new and inspired by Earl Derr Biggers' original character known to millions through the media of books, television and film, Charlie Chan, famed Honolulu sleuth, brings his inimitable talents to bear against danger, intrigue and death. A complete novel by Robert Hart Davis in each issue assures you of the best in mystery reading—regularly at your local newsstand!"
Charlie Chan Mystery Magazine No. 1, page 5

My introduction to Charlie Chan came in the late 1960s watching Warner Oland's portrayal of the character in movies on late-night television. Even then, the portrayal of African-American stereotypes in the films was offensive, but I didn't realize at the time that many Chinese-Americans were also offended by the presentation of Chan and his family members. A bit ironic in that Chan's creator, author Earl Derr Biggers (1884–1933), developed the character as a counterpoint to wicked Chinese characters like Fu Manchu and the media's Yellow Peril stereotypes of the day.

Unfortunately, the casting of whites like Swedish actor Oland and then American Sidney Toler as Chan only added to the on-screen insult. Nonetheless, I became a fast fan of the character, primarily due to Warner Oland's kindhearted, sagely performances.

Biggers first conceived of Charlie Chan after reading about Chinese-American police officer

Chang Apana of the Honolulu police force. Biggers' felt, "Sinister and wicked Chinese are old stuff, but an amiable Chinese on the side of law and order has never been done." Chan debuted in a supporting role in Biggers' mystery novel, *The House Without a Key*, in 1925.

A year later, Chan appeared onscreen in a ten-episode serial from Pathé Studios, based on the novel, portrayed by Japanese actor George Kuwa. In Biggers' second Chan novel, *The Chinese Parrot*, the great detective travels from Hawaii to California to solve the murder of a Chinese-speaking parrot and a servant. Universal Pictures filmed the novel in 1927, with a new Japanese actor, Kamiyama Sojin. The third novel, *Behind That Curtain*, was also filmed. This time by the Fox Film Corporation in 1929, starring Korean actor E.L. Park, but again Chan's role was minimal, and success was limited.

In 1931, the property finally gave Fox a bonafide hit, when it released *Charlie Chan Carries On*, based on Bigger's fifth Chan novel of the same name, with Warner Oland in the starring role. Sadly, only the Spanish-language version (*Eran Trece* "There Were Thirteen") of the film survives. Oland went on to star in 14 additional Chan films for Fox before his death in 1938. His last, *Charlie Chan in Monte Carlo*, was released in 1937.

The series was a huge success for Fox, taking in box office receipts at times comparable to A-List movies. It's credited with keeping the studio afloat during its lean depression-era years. Sidney Toler took over as the star of the series in 1939 and made 22 Chan films for

Fox, and later Monogram Studios. Upon his death in 1947, Roland Winters starred as Chan in six films for Monogram through 1949.

In 1971, Ross Martin played Chan in the TV-movie *The Return of Charlie Chan*, which wasn't aired until 1979. The most recent major motion picture was the comedic *Charlie Chan and the Curse of the Dragon Queen*, starring Peter Ustinov, Angie Dickinson, Roddy McDowall, and Michele Pfeiffer in 1981. Its cast of non-Chinese actors was controversial and was "an abysmal failure" at the box office.

A *Charlie Chan* comic strip appeared in 1938 but was ended abruptly by the McNaught Syndicate in May 1942 after the Japanese attack on Pearl Harbor. It was the first comic strip for Alfred Andriola (1912–1983), who later drew *Dan Dunn*, followed by the long-running *Kerry Drake*. You can read the Chan strip online at The Charlie Chan Family Home website

<charliechan.info/index.html>.

A 39-episode syndicated series called *The New Adventures of Charlie Chan*, produced by Television Programs of America, aired during the 1958/59 season in the United States. Based in England, the series was set in London and starred J. Carrol Nash as Chan. Unfortunately, ratings were poor and no additional seasons were produced. A tie-in comic book series of the same name debuted in 1958 from DC, lasting six issues.

Other comic book series include Prize Comics' *Charlie Chan* (1948) created by Joe Simon and Jack Kirby (five issues), Charlton Comics (1955, four issues), Dell Comics (1965, two issues), and Gold Key Comics' *The Amazing Chan and the Chan Clan* (1973, four issues), based on Hanna Barbera's Saturday morning cartoon series, which originally aired in Fall 1972, and reran in syndication through 1982. Chan was voiced by Key Luke, the actor who played "Number One Son" Lee Chan in several Chan films opposite Warner Oland, and one opposite Roland Winters.

On radio, Chan's adventures aired in several series broadcast from 1932 to 1948 on NBC's Blue Network, Mutual, and ABC. Walter Connolly was the first to play Chan on radio on Esso Oil's *Five Star Theater* for NBC's Blue Network in 1932. The program serialized Biggers first three novels in 30-minute episodes. Ed Begley, Sr. played Chan, with Leon Janney as Number One Son on NBC's *The Adventures of Charlie Chan* (1944–1948). Santos Ortega played the role of Chan in the series' final season.

Charlie Chan's first appearance in a digest magazine was actually in *Ellery Queen* May 1971. Jon L. Breen penned "The Fortune Cookie" for Queen himself. It's billed on the cover as a pastiche, but Charlie Chan appears as himself, not a cleverly named imitation. Breen's tightly plotted yarn concerns a Professor of Chinese Classics, suspected of killing a student whom he plagiarized in his latest book. When the student recognized his own work, he threatened to expose the Professor.

In 1956, Leo Margulies launched Renown Publications with *Michael Shayne Mystery Magazine* (shortened to "Mike" from April 1957 on). *Mike Shayne* went on to become one of the most successful digest magazines ever published, appearing on newsstands every month for nearly 30 years. The Renown line also garnered various levels of success with *The Man from U.N.C.L.E.*, *The Girl from U.N.C.L.E.*, *Shell Scott Mystery Magazine*, *Satellite Science Fiction*, and revivals of *Short Stories*, *Weird Tales*, and *Zane Grey Western*. The last new title from Renown was *Charlie Chan Mystery Magazine*, which debuted in November 1973 and ended after four issues in August 1974.

Like Renown's other character-based series, each issue of *Charlie Chan* opened with a new "novel" featuring the title detective. These were actually novelettes or "short novels" as they were called in *Mike Shayne*. The Chan novels were credited to Robert Hart Davis, a house name Margulies often used in magazines like his U.N.C.L.E. series.

The real Robert Davis gave Margulies his start in publishing when he hired him to work on staff at *Munsey's Magazine* in 1919. "Leo was so grateful for Davis' early support that he honored him years later using "Robert Hart Davis" as a pseudonym in two of his 1960s pulp magazines. He felt Davis was the greatest editor that ever lived."[1] Margulies' wife and partner since 1937, Cylvia Kleinman, "once said that the "Hart" came about because of Robert Davis' kind heart."[2]

The editorial credits in *Charlie Chan* list Margulies as publisher and Kleinman as editorial director. Thom Montgomery was added to the masthead as editor in issues three and four. Montgomery served concurrently as the editor for *Mike Shayne* from April 1974 to April 1975.

All four *Charlie Chan* covers were painted by Bill Edwards. Each captures a scene from that issue's Chan "novel," and each was later repurposed—sometimes more than once—for *Mike Shayne.*

Renown magazines were generous in their use of interior illustrations. Unfortunately, unless signed by the artist, the artwork is uncredited. The Chan stories, in particular, ran as many as a dozen illustrations, often portraits of the cast of characters sprinkled throughout the stories. A few illos of Chan were repurposed from one issue to the next.

Alias Robert Hart Davis

Michael L. Cook, in *Mystery, Detective, and Espionage Magazines*, lists the following authors writing as Robert Hart Davis:

Charlie Chan No. 3 "The Temple of the Golden Horde" by Dennis Lynds

Charlie Chan No. 4 "The Pawns of Death" likely by Bill Pronzini and Jeff Wallman

Charlie Chan No. 1 Nov. 1973
Cover by Bill Edwards

Charlie Chan Mystery Magazine No. 1 Nov. 1973

In "Walk Softly, Stranger," Chan visits Los Angeles and uncovers the murder of Mei T'ang Wu, an aging Hollywood star with a valuable collection of jeweled insects and jadecraft. This 1970s version of Chan is updated to give the character greater depth and introspective.

> *"To Chan, there was nothing romantic about murder. It was dirty and all to often meant interminable toil before a murderer was brought to justice. Not infrequently, Chan had wondered, after dealing with a most atrocious killing, if the very filth whose cleansing was his job had not rubbed off on his own psyche. He who digs in dirt seldom keeps clean fingernails."*

Chan retains his calm manner and ancestral wisdom but now speaks fluent English, reverting

Mike Shayne Jan. 1981
Repurposed cover by Bill Edwards

to pidgin English only when it serves to disarm suspects or dispel wisdom drawn from one of his three principal mentors, Confucius, Lao Tse, and Li Tai Po.

The Chan short novel runs 68 pages, with the balance of the digest filled with short stories,

Bill Edwards' Repurposed Covers

Charlie Chan No. 1 Nov. 1973
- ☐ *Mike Shayne* Jan. 1981

Charlie Chan No. 2 Feb. 1974
- ☐ *Mike Shayne* Sep. 1976
- ☐ *Mike Shayne* May 1978
- ☐ *Mike Shayne* Mar. 1980

Charlie Chan No. 3 May 1974
- ☐ *Mike Shayne* Apr. 1978
- ☐ *Mike Shayne* Apr. 1980

Charlie Chan No. 4 Aug. 1974
- ☐ *Mike Shayne* Apr. 1982

many by writers familiar to readers of 1970s mystery magazines.

The Siesta Special
by Robert W. Alexander

Robert William Alexander (1905–1980) sold nearly two dozen short stories, most published in the 1960s in *Suspense* (UK), *Alfred Hitchcock*, and *Mike Shayne*. Tension revs up quickly in "The Siesta Special," when a bus driver is confronted by an oddly disguised passenger with a mysterious box he claims contains a bomb. Extortion ensues as the purpose behind the threat slowly emerges. By the end, justice is unexpectedly served.

She Waits by Andrew Bogen

Galactic Central lists only two stories for Andrew Bogen. The first: "Black Powder" for *Mike Shayne* (Dec. 1972), and the second: "She Waits." The tale is well-written, and its action moves along at a crisp pace. The plot is drawn from technology that was relatively new in 1973. Unfortunately, the author uses a similar-sounding word for this technology, that means something entirely different. It's not enough to spoil a good story but certainly deflates the big reveal after its carefully constructed build-up.

Buttermilk by Bill Pronzini

A cantankerous couple can't keep an uncivil word to themselves. Pronzini piles on a dead-end job, irritating neighbors, and oppressive heat. When hubby steps outside one evening to clear his head, instead, his stress only mounts:

> *"My head feels like it's going to explode, he thought. The proverbial rat race at the office today, work backlogged, those*

secretaries chattering like a bunch of wind-up squirrels; I can still hear them even now. And then the freeway traffic, all those gleaming metal monsters, their horns braying and their brakes screaming. Oh yes, and we can't forget this omnipresent heat, two months now, two months with no relief in sight; God, now I know what a chicken feels like on a barbecue spit . . ."

As his world devolves, he cracks like an egg dropped on a granite countertop and makes headline news in the morning's paper.

Bernard and the Bust of His Father by Pauline C. Smith

Pauline Coggeshall Smith (1908–1994) wrote several dozen stories for *Alfred Hitchcock* and a few for *Mike Shayne* from 1968 to 1983. Her work appears twice in *Charlie Chan*. In this story, the titular Bernard is a tyrant, and as his poor wife tells the tale, she's the brunt of his tyranny. Thursdays are his club night, so she uses her one solo evening of the week to dream about his life-altering termination.

"These Thursday nights have become so filled with punctilious deliberation upon murder that it is now difficult for me to separate reality from imaginative planning. I have paid such particular attention to every detail that I sometimes wonder—is it happening or is it yet to happen?"

Coincidentally, Robert Arthur wrote "The People Next Door" under the pseudonym Pauline C. Smith for *The Mysterious Traveler Magazine* June 1952 [see *TDE2* page 46].

Death on Deck by Jim Duke

When Webe Devaney turns up dead in the truck yard, his pal Marcus "Yak" Aborn can't help asking questions. His boss, Lassiter, suggests he leave things to the police. Marcus is jumped at his apartment, but he's a big man and recovers, while his two assailants escape. The next day he's canned. Lassiter claims one of the other truck drivers complained about him.

The plot thickens nicely as Marcus uncovers a crime that somebody thinks is worth murdering to keep hidden.

Going Straight by George Antonich

Two career thieves drive a load of stolen appliances along the Coast Highway, from Frisco to L.A. Along the way, we learn Kidd wants out of this life of crime. The stake he'll receive, once Brokaw unloads the goods in L.A., will be enough to live on while he pursues his dream of writing. Brokaw, on the other hand, loves his life of crime and is already thinking about his next job. He also has a vendetta against drinking—years before, a drunk driver ended his football career prematurely, just as the NFL was in sight.

As they snake along the twisting, cliffside highway a hard-top careens past, its horn blaring. Kidd can see Brokaw's anger rise as the hard-top swerves from one side of the road to the other, and disappears around a curve. Fuming, Brokaw wants to catch the no-good drunk and pound some sense into his head, but the truck is no match for the fleet hard-top. He'll have to settle for calling it in from the phone booth Kidd tells him is coming up at the

Charlie Chan No. 2 Feb. 1974
Cover by Bill Edwards

observation lookout dead ahead.

When they reach it, the hard-top has crashed, toppling the phone booth, its engine smoking as it teeters on the edge of the cliff. Before Kidd can stop him, Brokaw nudges the truck into the car, pushing it over the cliff.

The pair proceeds to Salinas, but whatever trust they once shared went over the precipice like the hard-top.

The Innocent One

by Lawrence Treat

Charlie Chan included work by its share of prolific writers like Lawrence Treat (1903–1998), who is credited as a pioneer of police procedurals. Long before Sue Grafton, Treat wrote a series of "alphabet novels" such as *B as in Banshee* (1940), although he cherry-picked the letters to fit his plots. Treat was a founding member of the Mystery Writers of America and two-time winner of the Edgar Award.

In "The Innocent One," a con man discovers the new partner he's been searching for in a chance meeting at a department store. After a series of tests, she wins his confidence, and together they embark on a series of cons leading up to "the big one." Things move along swimmingly until a cascade of misjudgments turns the con man back into a con.

Charlie Chan Mystery Magazine No. 2 Feb. 1974

In "The Silent Corpse," Chan is on the island of Hawaii to attend the funeral of Lionel Burdon, the leader of one of the great families of the island state. Chan "had been known long and favorably to the deceased, having attained the status of valued friend after managing to restore safely to her home the kidnapped Lenore Burdon not merely unharmed but without payment of ransom."

After the funeral, Chan and Burdon's physician drive to the family estate where they soon become stranded, along with several family members, by an impending hurricane. Burdon's death is ruled a suicide, but Chan is puzzled as to motive, whereas several family members will directly profit from Burdon's passing.

Like the Chan films, the cast in "Silent Corpse" is large, providing plenty of suspects. However, introducing all the characters and their relationships requires a fair amount of backstory, which keeps the opening chapters a bit slow. Fortunately, the pace quickens once everyone is "on stage."

Unlike the movies, the final

showdown between Chan and the murderer takes place one-on-one, rather than in a drawing room where all the suspects have gathered. The series update for contemporary times (c. 1974) is nowhere more visible than in the casual sex between characters, which barely ruffles even Chan.

Figure in Flight by John Lutz

A hitman reads the obituary of a man whom he'd recently killed. Then he swears he glimpses the man on the street. He calls him on the phone but receives no response. He visits the man's house, which appears deserted. Then he spots the man driving a car and tails him. Is it really him, or is the hitman losing his grip on reality?

John Lutz (1939–) sold his first story to *Alfred Hitchcock's Mystery Magazine* in Dec. 1966. He went on to write numerous novels and over a hundred short stories. He was interviewed in the Summer 1979 issue of *The Armchair Detective.* In 1982, his "Ride the Lightning" became the first story from *Alfred Hitchcock* to win an Edgar Award. In the 60th anniversary issue of the digest (Dec. 2016) Lutz was invited to reminisce about the magazine and wrote in part, "To keep the short story flame flickering is a pleasure. To pass the torch an honor."

And the Beast was Marked
by Hal Ellson

A few of the supporting stories in *Charlie Chan* feature series characters like Chan himself. One was Hal Ellson's Victor Fiala who works for the explosive Captain Meza. Fiala is less reactive and more contemplative than his boss. The

Mike Shayne Sep. 1976
Repurposed cover by Bill Edwards

character first appeared in *Mike Shayne* in May 1963, then moved to *The Saint* and *Shell Scott* for several adventures, and ended his career in the pages *Mike Shayne.*

In "And the Beast was Marked" two teenage girls have been murdered, both struck from behind and then strangled with a strand of sisal. Fiala soon connects the double homicide with an earlier killing in a small village north of Montes. Fiala's progress on the case is largely due to fortuitous clues that practically land in his lap. But he's an affable character and shines when interviewing suspects and witnesses. He eventually triumphs but not before another victim falls prey to the killer.

Early on, Hal Ellson (1910–1994) was a ward at Bellevue Hospital and began writing about teenage gangs, drawn from his institutional experience at Bellevue in the 1940s. His first novel *Duke* in 1949, garnered the attention of the press and was followed by *Tomboy* (1950) about a girl gang leader. The 1957 Bantam edition proclaims "Over 1,000,000 Copies in Print." It eventually sold over four times that and was the basis for *Terrain Vague* (*Wasteland*) by French director Marcel Carne in 1960. Ellson continued writing novels about juvies and punks throughout his career but was also a prolific short story writer. His work appeared in *Manhunt*, *The Saint Detective Magazine*, *Shell Scott Mystery Magazine*, *Alfred Hitchcock's Mystery Magazine*, and many others.

A Payment for Murder

by James P. Cody

Bobby Joe Taylor is a hit man, trained and frequently contracted by a crime syndicate. He's good at his job and knows it, which leads him to a rate increase. But when a rival gang learns his assignment procedure and hires him to rub out one of the syndicate's own, the boss is forced to teach Bobby Joe a permanent lesson.

Cody gives Bobby a believable backstory tracing the killer's rise from errand boy to hitman, and the blow-by-blow of his final hit keeps the story moving.

James P. Cody (1926–2004) changed his name to Peter Thomas Rohrbach after his parents died and the Rohrbach family adopted him. He joined the Catholic Carmelite Order in 1948 and was ordained as a priest in 1952. He wrote several religious texts during his priesthood. He married Sheila Sheehan four years after leaving the priesthood in 1966.

Rohrbach went on to write fiction under his original name. He published one story each in *Mike Shayne*, *Alfred Hitchcock*, and *Charlie Chan*. He also wrote the four book series "The D.C. Man" for Berkley Medallion, 1974–1975.

Victor Fiala Stories by Hal Ellson

- ☐ "The Marrow of Justice" *Mike Shayne* May 1963
- ☐ "Shadows in the Sun" *The Saint* (UK) Aug. 1964
- ☐ "Up on the Mountain" *The Saint* April 1965
- ☐ "A Small Sin" *Shell Scott* March 1966
- ☐ "And the Beast was Marked" *Charlie Chan* Feb. 1974
- ☐ "A Night to Kill" *Mike Shayne* June 1974
- ☐ "Ride to the Killing" *Mike Shayne* July 1974
- ☐ "A Piece of Rope" *Mike Shayne* July 1975
- ☐ "A Needle in the Haystack" *Mike Shayne* Nov. 1975

Thou Shalt Not by Henry Slesar

Paradise is swept from a downtrodden American named Munger when he accepts a job from a Polynesian chieftain. Religion forbids the taking of a life by a native on the atoll known as Suva Oa—but not by an outsider. Slesar builds tension thick enough to cut with the razor edge of a sacrificial sword in this terrific tale of suspense billed as "a story you won't soon forget."

Henry Slesar (1927–2002) wrote hundreds of SF, fantasy, and mystery stories. His scripts include episodes for *The Twilight Zone*, *The Man from U.N.C.L.E.*, and *Alfred Hitchcock Presents*. His most collectible digest story was his novelization of *20 Million Miles to Earth* for *Amazing Stories Science Fiction Novel* No. 1 in 1957 [*TDE7* pgs 38 & 42].

A Walk On the Beach

by Lawrence Treat

Opportunist Arthur Emery

plans to marry Bambi Unger. She's aware he once embezzled ten grand and managed to stay out of jail when he paid it all back. He's aware she's the sole heir of her wealthy Uncle Mercer Unger. So when the opportunity to speed up her inheritance appears, Arthur takes it and bashes in Mercer's head during a walk on the beach.

Night Voice by M.G. Ogan

Winner of the issue's most interesting premise:

> *"Special Complaints is a one-man police department division set up by St. Petersburg's Chief of Police, Fred Anselmo. He tagged me, Lieutenant Gil Baker, to handle the nuts and cranks who plague police work."*

The late wife of Kiddie TV Show host Little Timmy is haunting his dreams, urging him to commit suicide so he can join her in the hereafter. If he does, his current wife inherits the Little Timmy fortune—a not inconsiderable amount. LT only gets the message at night, hence the title. I loved the premise and the supernatural dilemma that opens this story. Unfortunately, Ogan devised a rational explanation for everything, including the motive (the inheritance) that wasn't quite as stimulating.

Dinner With the Boss
by Edward D. Hoch

A four-pager in which our hero goes to dinner at the boss' house hoping it'll lead to a promotion with the company. Readers soon learn it's a setup to arrest our erstwhile hero.

Edward D. Hoch was born in Rochester, New York in 1930. He sold his first story in 1955

Charlie Chan No. 3 May 1974
Cover by Bill Edwards

and became a full-time writer in 1968. Although he wrote several novels, his published short stories numbered nearly 1,000 at the time of his death in 2008.

Charlie Chan Mystery Magazine No. 3 May 1974

For me, the best Chan story appeared in the third issue: "The Temple of the Golden Horde." ("Horde" is incorrectly replaced by "Death" on the contents page.)

Like the previous stories, this one begins with a murder. Benny Chan, a sweet young man with cognitive disabilities, works for the Khan of the Temple of the Golden Horde. He nearly reaches the Temple in San Francisco, to deliver the fifth scroll of six, he's brought from Hawaii when he's beset by demons and found drowned the next day. Officially his death is

Mike Shayne April 1978
Repurposed cover by Bill Edwards

deemed an accident, but at least one person—the victim's sister Betty Chan—won't accept it. She appeals to Charlie Chan, whom she learns is visiting San Francisco for the International Penology Symposium, as an attendee and presenter. This time Chan's pidgin English has been dropped entirely. It's wisely transferred to another character, C.V. Soong, a great historian of Chinese, scholar, benefactor, and philanthropist. Soong is from Hawaii like Chan; only he's in town to recover the scroll Benny was carrying.

The Chinese scrolls and Temple add an exotic layer of atmosphere and mystery to the story. Locally, the Temple has its share of controversy, but its leaders maintain it's a haven for misguided youth. In reality, it's an expensive cultish prison where rich people dump their out-of-control children to have them whipped back into shape. And as Chan uncovers, it's a front for a drug smuggling operation.

The plot here is on par with the earlier novels, but the writing, action, and overall feel of the story are superior. It's also the most successful story in terms of updating Chan's character for modern times.

A Verdict of Death by John Lutz

Frank Seabold is accused, arrested, and tried for the murder of his wife, Nina. Besides being loaded, Frank's wife also has a big insurance policy, so the jury understands there's a strong potential motive. But police can't produce a body despite digging up Seabold's basement and yard. There is simply no trace of Mrs. Seabold. An excellent story with a great twist, and a nasty ending.

Your Money or Your Life
by James Holding

After fourteen operations, Flaglar is still unable to walk without crutches. He's depressed and tired, and simply wants to end it all, but hasn't got the stomach to pull the trigger himself. Instead, he cooks up a scheme to hire someone else to do it for him. All he needs is a complete stranger with no prior connection, to ensure their safety after the deed is done.

James Holding (1907–1997) wrote over 100 short stories for *Alfred Hitchcock*, *Ellery Queen*, and *Mike Shayne*. His Queen pastiche series, with King Danforth and Martin Leroy writing as "Leroy King," include ten adventures, all published in *EQMM*. *The Zanzibar Shirt Mystery and Other Stories* (Crippen & Landru, 2018) reprints them all.

Nose Job by Syd Hoff

Al and Shirley are con artists with a history. They lost track of each other years ago. Now Shirley's old eagle beak is an upturned button nose. When Al runs into her at the Emerald Beach Hotel, he joins her and her latest mark, a wealthy older gentleman named Mr. Ostrach. She's ready to cut Al in on her profits, but can a con ever really trust another con?

Syd Hoff (1912–2004) is best remembered for his cartoons and children's books, including those about Danny and the Dinosaur.

Cop on the Run by David Mazroff

Another series character, David Mazroff's PI Rick Harper, wraps up his final case in "Cop on the Run." Although Harper was based in San Francisco, this time he's hired to find the missing daughter of millionaire Howard Sloane in Detroit. Ilene's disappearance could be tied to a series of abduction/murders so Harper teams with the local police department. His help is eschewed by Detective O'Connell in missing persons but welcomed by homicide detective Mike Carmody, who openly shares his files on four previous murders that may be related to Ilene's disappearance. The fact that one of the earlier victims was O'Connell's wife adds an interesting twist to the case.

David Mazroff wrote dozens of true crime articles, along with a few stories, for *Mike Shayne Mystery Magazine* from 1968 through 1977. His first fiction sale was to *Guilty Detective Story Magazine* in Dec. 1961.

Rick Harper Stories by David Mazroff

- ☐ "The Snatch of Shirley Kale"
  Mike Shayne April 1973
- ☐ "The Disappearing Trucks"
  Mike Shayne Sep. 1973
- ☐ "Cop on the Run"
  Charlie Chan No. 3 May 1974

Mike Shayne April 1980
Repurposed cover by Bill Edwards

Incident in Three Crossings by Jack Foxx

A novice counterfeiter has mapped out a series of small towns to drop his newly minted twenty dollar bills. Too bad the locals are experts who don't take kindly to amateur competition. At about five pages, the story adequately fills its role as a short, short story.

The prolific author Bill Pronzini wrote under the pseudonym Jack Foxx, primarily in *Alfred Hitchcock*.

Button, Button by Evelyn Payne

Returning from his imprisonment during the Vietnam War, Wyn stays with his Aunt Fay whom he

Charlie Chan No. 4 Aug. 1974
Cover by Bill Edwards

hasn't lived with since before the war. He and his cousins, Harvey and Val, recall Aunt Fay's collection of gemstone buttons, and now realize these valuables shouldn't be kept in her home. Wyn's concern grows when a neglected cigarette starts a fire in his room, and his squeeze ball nearly causes Fay to fall on the stairs—and he's certain he wasn't responsible for either.

Evelyn Cameron Payne (1907–1977) wrote a half dozen stories for *Alfred Hitchcock* and one for *Mike Shayne*.

Deadly Prescription

by Herbert Harris

A young doctor begins his career when he joins a middle-aged mentor's practice. It isn't long until the youngster tires of the older man's controlling behavior and falls in love with his partner's much younger wife. He sees an opportunity to poison the old man and thinks he'll take it. Nice twist ending, but getting there is a little forced.

Herbert Harris (1911–1995) sold two stories to *Espionage Magazine* in the mid-1980s, and one to *Combat: The Action Magazine* in April 1957. His "The Wall Game" first appeared in *Argosy* (UK) in Oct. 1970, and was reprinted in *Espionage* Feb. 1985.

Charlie Chan Mystery Magazine No. 4 August 1974

Chan's adventure in his final issue is "The Pawns of Death." In this case, Chan is vacationing in Paris to attend the Transcontinental Chess Tournament. He's accompanied by Prefect Claude DeBevre, whom he'd met earlier during a crime conference in San Francisco. Chan stays at the Frontenac Hotel on the same floor as the chess tourney headliners, three-time champion, Lord Roger Mountbatten and rising star Grant Powell. The Swiss referee is Hans Dorner.

Mountbatten's wealthy backer is Clive Kettridge. Powell's friend and advisor is Raymond Balfour. The hostility between the players is equalled or exceeded by their associates.

Also on hand are reporter Tony Sprague, Clive's daughter, Jennifer Kettridge, Grant's wife Laura Powell, and Melvin Randolph, the player Grant Powell defeated to earn his spot in the Transcontinental.

With a cast of nine, plus the detectives, there are enough characters—even after two are killed off—to leave a good number of suspects. Indeed, Raymond Balfour is the first victim, alone in his hotel room, killed by a ball bearing "bullet," transforming this adventure into a locked-room mystery. Not much later, Tony Sprague is also murdered, this time with the fruit knife the hotel provides for its fruit baskets.

Although Chan drops several quotes of wisdom throughout the story his pidgin English is otherwise thankfully absent.

A Friend in Need by Al Nussbaum

After a stretch of bad luck, ex-con Joe happens upon his old cellmate, Pete, and enlists his aid in a heist. "It was a small bank, but because of large windows it was almost completely exposed to passersby." Turning a problem into an opportunity, the pair use a camera and its flashbulbs to blind any nosy pedestrian as to what's going on inside the bank during their heist. The plot seems plausible, but what develops soon backfires on poor old Joe.

Albert Frederick Nussbaum (1934–1996) was a bank robber before he was a writer. He killed a guard in Brooklyn, New York and fled to an apartment in Philadelphia, posing as a writer to cover the fact that he was unemployed while living off the loot. *The Name of the Game is Death* by Dan Marlowe struck Nussbaum as authentic, so he tracked Marlowe down and called him up, asking for writing tips.

Phone records indicated the two men talked often enough that the FBI appeared on Marlowe's doorstep after Nussbaum's mother-in-law tipped off authorities he was back in New York visiting his wife and infant daughter. Marlowe had no idea, yet the unusual relationship continued. Sentenced to 40 years in Leavenworth, Nussbaum sent stories to Marlowe in Michigan, and the

Mike Shayne April 1982
Repurposed cover by Bill Edwards

two writers shared advice. Marlowe on writing, Nussbaum on crime.

When he finally was paroled, Nussbaum was writing full time and never returned to his earlier life of crime. Over two dozen of Nussbaum's short stories were published in *Alfred Hitchcock* from 1967 to 1977, and he wrote scripts for episodes of TV's *Switch*, starring Robert Wagner and Eddie Albert.

The Exchange
by Ronald Anthony Cross

A Russian assassin approaches his target in a bar and strikes up an existential conversation.

"The Exchange" was Cross' (1937–2006) second published story and the only one to appear in a mystery magazine. His mainstay was science fiction and fantasy, and his resume includes work in *F&SF, Weird Tales*, and *Asimov's*. He wrote four novels in the 1990s for Tor Books.

"*Lake County Incidents* is like the Winesburg, Ohio of the weird and wretched. Cizak's precise and simple prose proves the most horrifying thing an author can show readers is a mirror."
- Marc E. Fitch, author of *Paradise Burns*

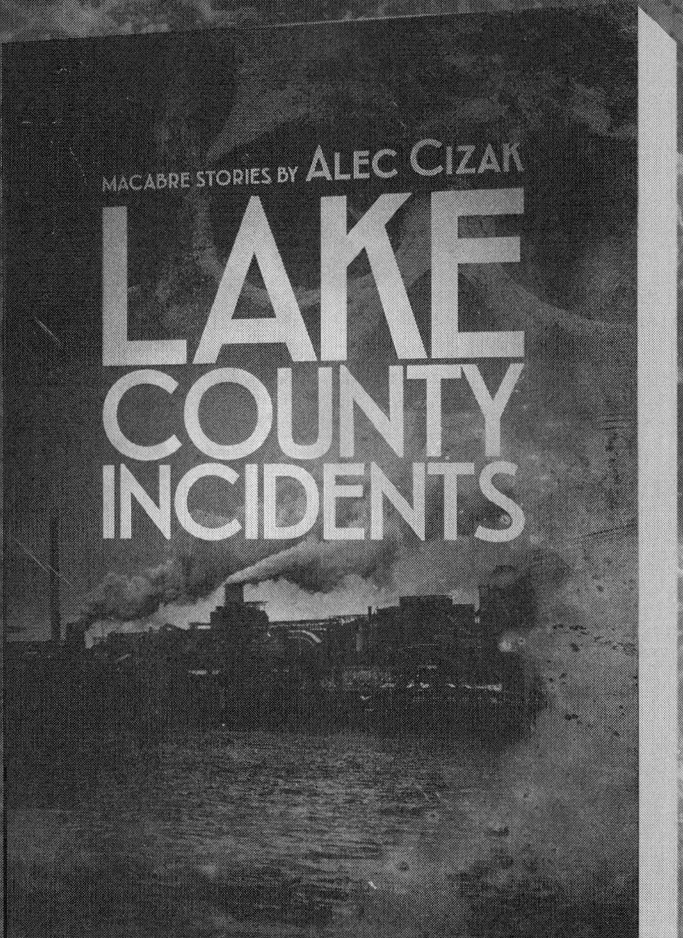

ABC
GROUP DOCUMENTATION

Summer
2019

Turn and Turn About
by Francis Clifford

Great heist caper with plenty of twists. A jewel thief forces a circus aerialist and her boyfriend to rob the cliffside manor of a wealthy woman. For their troubles, the thief allows his new partners to walk away empty-handed. His clever plan goes smoothly until the getaway when the twists begin.

Francis Clifford was a pseudonym of Arthur Leonard Bell Thompson (1917–1975), a British writer of crime stories and thrillers. He began writing full time in 1959 and produced 18 novels before his death—two that were published posthumously. His short stories appeared in *Argosy*, *Cosmopolitan*, and *Playboy*. "Turn About" was his only appearance in a mystery digest.

The Man Who Understood Women by Gary Brandner

David Carmody is every woman's dream; handsome and remarkably attentive. But he's not particularly successful at earning a living, so he jumps at the chance to marry a wealthy older woman, Elizabeth, whose doctor gives her five years to live. But three years into her death march, a miracle cure appears, and she's suddenly headed for a long life. Carmody does his best to stick it out but falling for twenty-something, gorgeous, Mavis, his wife's nurse, begins his life of crime and its unintended consequences.

Gary Brandner (1930–2013) is perhaps best known for his werewolf trilogy *The Howling*. He wrote over 30 novels and more than 100 short stories over his career, primarily horror. He sold his first story to *Ellery Queen* in 1969, that appeared in the July 1970 issue. His stories continued to appear regularly in *Ellery Queen*, *Alfred Hitchcock*, and *Mike Shayne* throughout the 1970s, tapering off by the early 1980s.

The subject of "Mike Shayne Mystery Makers" in Nov. 1979, he wrote, "Hobbies include strumming a cat and petting my guitar. I favor Tanqueray martinis, and I have enough old radio programs on tape to play day and night for five days . . ."

Murder Candidate by M.G. Ogan

Billed as a novelet, starring Wayne Morgan as a PI working for "a few defense attorney clients," this story takes its time introducing its characters and their interwoven relationships. Morgan is the former Sheriff of Thomasville, the hub of the St. Denis parish below New Orleans on the Mississipi. When Evelyn Ganey, editor of the *St. Denis Watchman* weekly newspaper, turns up dead, Morgan starts investigating. He's careful to respect local law enforcement, who eventually share information with him. Character relationships and history take several pages to establish, so the first half moves slowly. But once the stage is set, the pace quickens, and the story ends with a satisfying finish.

M.G. Ogan was a pseudonym for Margaret (1923–1979) and George Ogan (1912–1983). The pair wrote over two dozen stories for *Argosy*, *Mike Shayne*, *Alfred Hitchcock*, *Zane Grey*, *Ed McBain's*, and *The Executioner* from 1966–1978. Before that, as Lee Castle, George wrote three stories for *Gent* and *Adventure* men's magazines.

The Spider by Clarence Alva Powell

Charlie Chan Returns by Dennis Lynds
Bantam 1974 Charlie Chan Mystery No. 4

It's unclear whether the Spider is a vigilante or an assassin from a rival gang, but Sam Hardin and his men grow ever more fearful as their numbers dwindle, picked off one or two at a time. Although the Spider never appears until the final scene, he dominates every page as tension builds toward the climax.

Powell also wrote a couple of stories for *Mike Shayne* in the 1970s.

The Obituary by Pauline C. Smith

> *"Orin Coleman as a good obituary writer. His files of the great and near-great were always ready to add the most recent salient facts in case of sudden demise."*

Coleman's assistant Kenneth Camp does all the legwork, while Coleman does all the composition. The pair's careers run into years with Camp intent on the day he will replace his mentor. His first solo assignment: Orin Coleman.

Despite a full page ad inside the front cover urging readers to subscribe, *Charlie Chan* No. 4 was the final issue. Perhaps the page count—128—down from the previous 160, offered a clue to the magazine's fate. Another ad for the next issue announced "A thrilling new Mongo Fredrickson novelet" "Tiger in the Snow" by George C. Chesbro.

Mongo the Magnificent, a PI and former circus acrobat, was featured in a series of 14 novels by George C. Chesbro (1940–2008). *Playboy* described the series as ". . . Raymond Chandler meets Stephen King by way of Alice's looking glass." "Tiger" slated for *Chan* No. 5, shifted to *Mike Shayne,* appearing in the March 1976 issue.

Charlie Chan Returns

Around the same time Chan's magazine appeared, Bantam Books had begun reprinting Earl Derr Biggers original novels. A new motion picture was being readied for production. The screenplay for *Charlie Chan Returns* by Ed Spielman and Howard Friedlander was complete, and Dennis Lynds was hired to write the novelization. Although the movie was never made, Lynds completed the book, and Bantam published it as the fourth novel in their seven-book Chan series. (All the others were reprints of Earl Derr Biggers' original six novels.)

After reading Dennis Lynds' excellent Chan novelette in *Charlie Chan* No. 3, my expectations of

Charlie Chan Returns were high. Unfortunately, I suspect the source material hamstrung Lynds. Chan is vacationing in New York City and is quickly drawn into a murder case. He attends a dinner party hosted by wealthy philanthropist, Victor Cosmo, who shares a tape recording of a death threat. Besides Chan, everyone in attendance has been marginalized by Cosmo with reason(s) to want him dead. By outing everyone in the presence of the eminent Hawaiian detective, Cosmo figures his would-be killer will be deterred. Not so. The smug philanthropist is killed in his boobytrapped shower the following morning.

Chan's pidgin English is back in full force. Was it a factor that contributed to the screenplay never being filmed? It couldn't have helped. On the plus side, Chan's Number Three son, Jimmy Chan, speaks flawless English and is a police detective for New York City. Unlike the Oland/Toiler movies, here Chan's son gets to play it straight from start to finish.

Charlie Chan Mystery Magazine's Final Cases

Before the *Charlie Chan* folded, its editors had two more Chan adventures in the can. "The City of Brotherly Death" was originally announced for issue No. 3, but never appeared. The story was recast as an adventure for Mike Shayne and appeared in *MSMM* May 1975, retaining its original title. Galactic Central credits Sam Merwin, Jr. as the author.

The large cast of "Brotherly Death," and the way the story unfolds, align with previous Chan stories, but its hard-boiled tone required more rework than simply changing Chan to Shayne. The story takes Shayne (Chan) from Miami (Honolulu) to Philadelphia at the request of an old friend, now a successful TV executive. The Mar-Bru conglomerate is packed with nepotism and dysfunction, and someone is siphoning millions from the corporate coffers, planting evidence so Shayne's friend will take the blame should the theft ever be discovered. It's an enjoyable adventure on par with the bulk of Chan's digest appearances, but for me, the hard-boiled edge gives it a little something extra.

Mike Shayne May 1975 with "The City of Brotherly Death" by Sam Merwin, Jr. recast for Mike Shayne

The final story, "Death on the Strip" by Gary Brandner, was scheduled for *Charlie Chan* No. 5. For the rework, Chan is transformed into a character named Sammy Chung ("Famous Oriental Detective") and queued up for *Mike Shayne*.

GREASEPAINT
&45s
EDITED BY RYAN SAYLES
FEATURING STORIES BY:
PATRICIA ABBOTT, J.L. ABRAMO,
JEN CONLEY, DAVID JAMES KEATON,
RICHARD THOMAS AND MORE

AVAILABLE NOW
FROM
DOWN & OUT
BOOKS
GREASEPAINT
&45s
EDITED BY RYAN SAYLES

Mike Shayne Dec. 1979 with "Death on the Strip" part one by Gary Brandner recast for Sammy Chung

Mike Shayne Jan. 19780 with "Death on the Strip" part two by Gary Brandner recast for Sammy Chung

Due to the novelette's length, it appeared in two part in *Mike Shayne* Dec. 1979 and Jan. 1980.

Like Dennis Lynds in *Charlie Chan* No. 3, Gary Brandner wisely introduces us to the story's cast as the tale unfolds, avoiding several chapters of backstory. Like all the Chan digest stories, this one opens with a murder. Only this time, it appears that jilted girlfriend Amy Tobin really did kill her callous lover, bad boy Joe Romo, at his bungalow on the grounds of the Oasis Hotel in Vegas.

The "Chung" name change is easy to ignore and enjoy this story as a Charlie Chan original. It rivals issue three's "The Temple of the Golden Horde" in quality, with "Chan" doing the majority of the investigation alongside Lieutenant Kagle of the Las Vegas police department. Collectors and fans would do well to add these two issues of *Mike Shayne* to their *Chan* digest collections. It was great to see this final piece of the *Charlie Chan Mystery Magazine* go out on a high note.

References

[1] *Leo Margulies: Giant of the Pulps* by Philip Sherman, pg 17 Altus Press, 2017

[2] *Leo Margulies: Giant of the Pulps* by Philip Sherman, pg 212 Altus Press, 2017

<dangerousdwarf.com>
<mysteryscenemag.com>
<otrcat.com>
<paperbackwarrior.com>
<philsp.com>
<queen.spaceports.com>
<thrillingdetective.com>
<washingtonpost.com>

The One, the Only, Bronze Books

Article by Steve Carper

A gossip item in the March 1963 *Negro Digest* reported that Robert Lucas' next book would be an interracial romance, *The Blacker the Berry*, and that he would follow that with his big novel at last, a study of interracial love in the suburbs tentatively titled *The Split-Level Plantation*.

In a quick game of word association, "bronze" probably brings to mind a third-place finish at the Olympics, or the age when copper and tin were alloyed together to make stronger weapons, or a bust sculptors make from the metal. In an earlier era, a fourth meaning might have predominated: bronze was a euphemism for black.

The South Side of Chicago, the home to the burgeoning African-American community, had been nicknamed Bronzeville in about 1930. The name caught on. Every year, a huge community event was the naming of the Mayor of Bronzeville, not a politician but a prominent citizen working in and for the neighborhood, and the crowning of Miss Bronze America, "the most beautiful Negro girl in the country," as the newspapers called her. Both events lasted for decades. The classic sociological study *Black Metropolis: A Study of Negro Life in a Northern City* by St. Clair Drake and Horace C. Cayton, published in 1945, explained the term in a way that inverts modern expectations:

> The expression "Bronze" when counterposed to "Black" reveals a tendency on

the part of Negros to avoid referring to themselves as "black." And, of course, as a descriptive term, the former is even more accurate than the latter, for most Negros *are* brown. [italics in original]

Whatever modern readers think of that explanation, "bronze" meant an immediately identifiable marker in 1952, the year in which the digest line Bronze Books lived and died.

The two Bronze Books were published by Designs Publishing

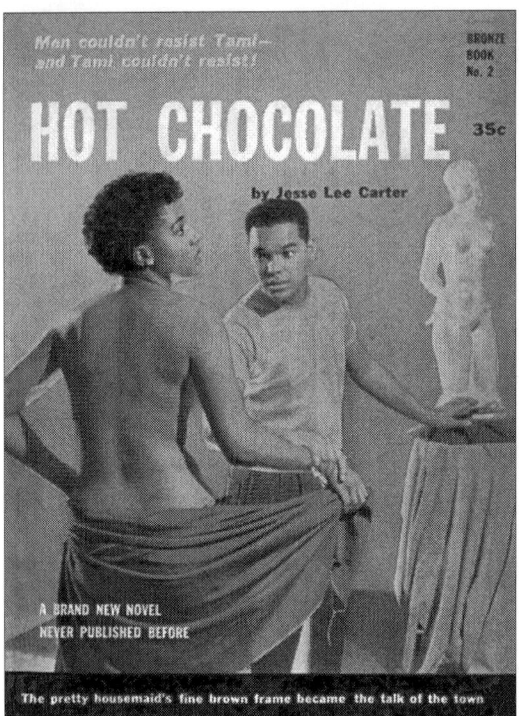

Company, about which no scraps of information have survived except that it is the listed publisher of the 55 digests released as Intimate Novels, also started in 1952. Both lines have a telltale clue hidden in plain sight. Those readers who wanted more of these normally 35¢ novels could send off a coupon for four similarly provocative titles for $1.00, nine for $2.00, or fourteen for $3.00 to Universal Publishing and Distributing Corp. UPD, as it's usually known, was Arnold Abramson's paperback conglomerate, also publishers of digest lines Uni-Books, Fiesta Books, and Stallion Books, all now clumped under the "sleaze" label, and the more mainstream Universal Giants, more like oversized mass-market paperbacks than true digests, though normally included in digest listings. Its titles like *Hussy*, *Dope Doll*, and *Forbidden Fruit* show the thin lines among sleaze, romance, and ordinary novels.

In the early 1950s, paperbacks, like virtually all other popular culture, were written by whites about whites. Covers were painted by white artists using white models. Sleaze offered a way to make black faces visible, although one that might politely be called ironic. Paperbacks—mostly mass-market paperbacks, which had after the war quickly turned to lurid covers and titles to boost sales—allowed some of the cover faces to be black if the books titillated readers with tales of interracial romance, light-skinned blacks "passing" for white (and leading to interracial affairs), miscegenation with slaves, whites among the natives (who, if female, could be shown with bare breasts), or the queasy inference of black rape. Of the 33 paperback covers I found showing black faces between 1947 and 1952 (less than 1% of titles published), only a handful depicted blacks in everybody life among blacks. Of those, exactly two were by black writers: Claude McKay's early Harlem Renaissance novel *Home to Harlem* (Avon 376, 1951) and Richard Wright's nonfiction memoir *Black Boy* (Signet 841, 1951).

Bronze Books exploded every one of these rules. Their books

were written by black authors about black people. Their covers were photos rather than paintings and the models were black. (The word "black" is nowhere to be found on the covers or the blurb material, to be sure. Neither are "colored" or "Negro." The women are "brown" and "bronze" and "dusky" and, wonderfully, "a dream the color of leaves turned golden-brown by the autumn sun," a phrase the blurb writer wisely stole from the text.) The titles were equally coded: Bronze Book No. 1 was *Harlem Model* as by "Luke Roberts" and Bronze Book No. 2 was *Hot Chocolate* as by "Jesse Lee Carter." ("As by?" Yes. I know Luke Roberts was a pseudonym and I'm pretty sure Jesse Lee Carter was too.) Both were "original novel[s] never before published in any form," unlike the many, often retitled, reprints that paperback publishers normally offered.

Evidence suggests that the books were released very late in 1952. Copyright registration can be made within 90 days of publication: while the official copyright date for both was 1952, the actual registration took place on January 6, 1953, with an "in notice: 1952" designation, meaning that they were submitted before the end of that year and not processed until January. UPD regularly paired a line's first two titles in some way, so the two may have been released together. The first two Fiesta Books share a copyright registration date. Two Universal Romance novels hit the stands before the line's name shortened to Uni-Book with No. 3.

The plot of *Harlem Model* is one long cliché. A young man, soon nicknamed "Ace," breaks up with his small-town girl, and flees to the big city of New York. There he's hustled by the city slickers, falls in love at first sight when he sees a photo shoot with a glamorous model named Fay, and fortuitously stumbles into a job that gives him access to the modeling community. He discovers a promising contender and winds up making a name for himself as a model's agent—in the company owned by Fay. Just when everything looks rosy, he learns that the whole business is a corrupt front, and almost loses everything when a surprising death occurs. He leaves the high life behind for the arms of his small-town sweetheart. Hollywood told variations on this tale a hundred times, starring whatever handsome, winsome, and toothsome young hopefuls they had under contract.

For its audience, the oft-told ordinariness of the plot wouldn't have been a detriment but a resounding triumph. The plot threads might be clichés but they were All-American clichés rather than the clichés of black exploitation. Nobody talks in dialect, no one ever bows to "massa." (Proving that the Beats stole their slang from black vocabulary, we see "daddy-o" and "dig" and "jive" for color alongside the perfectly grammatical English dialog.) Black characters fill every niche in society, from landlady to newspaper reporter to business owner to gangster. They can handle it all; whites are not needed in this ecology. The corruption is sleaze, admittedly: Fay's agency is a front for a prostitution ring; she has refused Ace's advances because she is the worst horror '50s audiences could imagine: a lesbian. All the sex is carefully off-page nevertheless and Ace, notwithstanding his panting

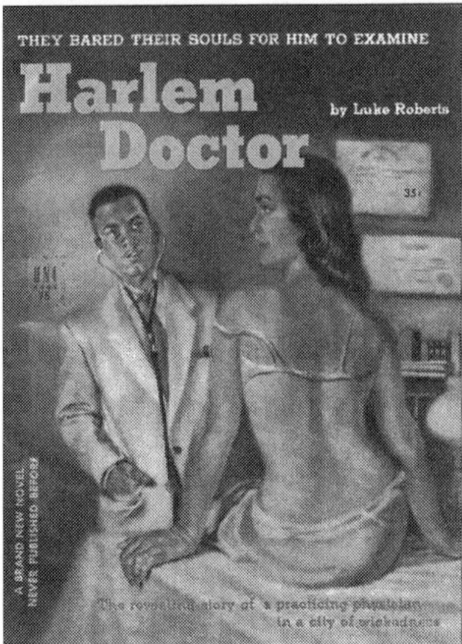

after Fay, is always looking for and finding romance. The book is not in any way colorblind, but it can be said to be color neutral: it is nothing special in the best possible way.

Hot Chocolate rides atop a different but equally Hollywood set of clichés. The impossibly beautiful Tami works to support Rip Tate, a genius sculptor, until he can be discovered by the art world. They are emotionally a couple, but Rip—a '50s male—refuses to marry until he can support a wife and children. Tami is the most understanding girlfriend in history: not only does she support him emotionally and financially, but she dismisses his dalliances with his models as part of his needs. Why doesn't she just be his model? Rip won't let her. A true artist, he maintains, needs flaws to activate his creativity and Tami is physically flawless. And lucky as well. Like Ace, she snags the perfect job, as maid to the wealthy and internationally acclaimed—and white —painter Meyerbloom. The ending is foretold, but the plot twists for a while to feature Meyerbloom's son, who is a jazz clarinetist so hot he gets a job with the black hepcats while panting futilely after Tami, and Bertha, the curvy model who desperately wants Rip to leave art, get a good job, and marry her. The elder Meyerbloom eventually sees the bounty placed in front of him; Tami's perfection is needed for the project he envisions. Tami offers a more intimate use of her body if he would look at even one of Rip's sculptures. He says yes—who in any sleaze novel wouldn't?—and anoints Rip as a genius. Then he gallantly refuses Tami's gift. In Hollywood, the movie ends there. In sleaze, never. Tami, a feminist in full control of her body, points out she's totally free until she takes her wedding vows and insists on fulfilling the deal. "She did her best for him . . ." That's as close to sex as the frustrated readers get.

While *Hot Chocolate* is also set in Harlem, the community is not much developed beyond a bar, a jazz club, and a church social. The white community and Meyerbloom's fantasy household are equally scanted, though. Carter is just a lesser author, minimally competent but not adroit. All the characters are flatter—more clichéd in the bad way—than Roberts' and the plot strands don't mesh as neatly. Still, the black experience is never caricatured. They are standard-issue Americans, striving for success at work, longing for family and romance, looking for that Hollywood happy ending, wanting it all.

I'm taking a chance by proclaiming Carter to be a black writer, but I find it unthinkable that Abramson would go to such lengths to launch a black series and not use black writers for the inaugural releases. Why the series never went beyond the two titles is an utter mystery. The simplest explanation is that newsstands wouldn't accept covers with black couples.

Yet that explanation is almost certainly wrong. UPD published three more books by Roberts in 1953 under the Uni-Book imprint. *Reefer Club* was issued as was Uni No. 49 (and reprinted as Stallion Books No. 213 in 1954) and *Harlem Doctor* was Uni No. 75. Both editions of *Reefer Club* featured an all-white cover cast, but *Harlem Doctor*'s cover is thematically identical to *Harlem Model* and clearly intended to be another Bronze Book, although Uni used an illustration rather than a photo. And then there's Uni No. 76, again thematically identical, the boxing novel *Below the Belt*, by Robert Lucas.

Did I just give something away? The *Catalog of Copyright Entries* preceded me. All three Roberts books are listed as pseudonyms under the heading of Lucas, Robert. All his books are among the rarest and most expensive digests, and therefore hardest to find. I was lucky to find both Bronze titles together for $100, although the condition of *Hot Chocolate* wasn't as good as I could have hoped. The last time *Reefer Club* was on eBay it sold for $500. Fine copies of *Harlem Doctor* and *Below the Belt* were in a 2015 catalog for $450 each. My reading copy of the *Below the Belt* was a steal at $15.00. If you're looking for bargains on these titles, beware of false sightings online. Jane Manning wrote *Reefer Girl* for rival Hanro Corp., issued as Cameo Books No. 330 and reprinted by Venus Books No. 175 and No. 183 as *Young Sinners*. Even though the covers for the Venus reprints clearly state the old title, you might see it online as *Reefer Club*. Conversely, Graham Holroyd's *Paperback Prices and Checklist* gives Uni No. 49 as *Reefer Girl*, possibly the source of the mistake.

Luke Roberts is falsely identified online as well. The normally reliable, although very old and unupdated, Pulptrader lists the author of *Harlem Model* as Luke Roberts

("Robert Ehrenzweig"). Ehrenzweig was an Austrian writer who took the name of Robert Lucas when he fled the Nazis and wound up in Britain. He is an impossible choice to write novels about Harlem life.

I think I've pinned down the real Robert Lucas. The clue came from reading *Below the Belt*. An older man acts as the manager for a youngster who's a prime contender as a boxer. They encounter the corruption in the boxing racket when they get bankrolled by gangsters. Still, the money rolls in, along with the women, and they are headed for a shot at the title when a surprise death almost loses them everything. The chastened boxer finds his real calling out of the limelight, as the athletic director of a boys' club. Although set in South Side Chicago and with the older man as the viewpoint character, the plot has exactly the same arc and beats as *Harlem Model*. The dialog is also similar, with articulate characters using proper grammatical speech and no dialect.

Now check out *Naked in Hollywood*. Young, beautiful, New York model Carla's intense ambition is to become a movie star. An agent sees she's a true contender. A chance encounter gets her onto a TV show and then a big budget movie, revealing to her the corruption behind the Hollywood glitter. She's willing to sell out her scruples in return for fame, but a surprise death seems to reverse all she's worked toward. *Naked in Hollywood* was a Lancer original paperback in 1962. It has an all-white cast and Carla wins her stardom in the end. Otherwise, its rhythms are identical to *Harlem Woman* and *Below the Belt*. The author? Bob Lucas.

That Bob Lucas is easy to find. *Negro Digest* in 1963 called *Naked in Hollywood* his fifth book. *Negro Digest* was launched in 1942 by Ben Burns of the famed African-American newspaper, the *Chicago Defender*. When Bob Lucas died, his obituary in the July 30, 1990 issue of *Jet* magazine reported that he had worked for the *Chicago Defender*. A Robert Lucas also wrote numerous articles for *Negro Digest*. I doubt I'm taking any great leap in pronouncing Luke Roberts, Robert Lucas, and Bob Lucas one and the same.

I couldn't find a conventional biography of Lucas, so here's what I do know.

Probably born in 1913, Lucas graduated from Central YMCA College in 1938. Central (which became Roosevelt University in 1945) was Chicago's home for minorities kept out of other colleges, including African-Americans, Jews, Asians, and, oddly, Catholics. He worked for the Federal Writers Project and wrote several chapters of a planned book to be called *The Negro in Illinois*, headed by black poet and novelist Anna Bontemps, which went unpublished when the FWP was canceled because of the war. Lucas got a more permanent slot with the *Chicago Defender*. Burns spoke glowingly of Lucas: "A sterling backstop staff member was bright-eyed gnome Robert Lucas, a slow talker and fast writer who was also a would-be radio script-writer." He soon accomplished that goal, writing weekly scripts for the Woman's Army Corps during the war and for a local radio show, *Democracy U.S.A.*, in 1946.

Lucas spoke equally glowingly of Bontemps in a letter after he won a writing grant from the Rosenwald Fund in 1948. "All I can say is thanks for the interest you've shown to me back in WPA days [Works Progress Administration, the agency that ran the Writers Project] and through the years. It meant a great deal to me because there have been many times I was convinced I'd never be a writer. Now I think maybe there's some hope for me."

Presumably, Lucas, like so many young writers before and since, wrote books like the Bronze and Uni novels as practice and wallet-padders while hoping to write the big novel that would bring him money and fame. Only a handful achieved that goal. Lucas went back to journalism. He wrote articles for *Negro Digest* for more than a decade, worked for the *Los Angeles Sentinel*, another black newspaper, eventually became West Coast editor for *Jet*

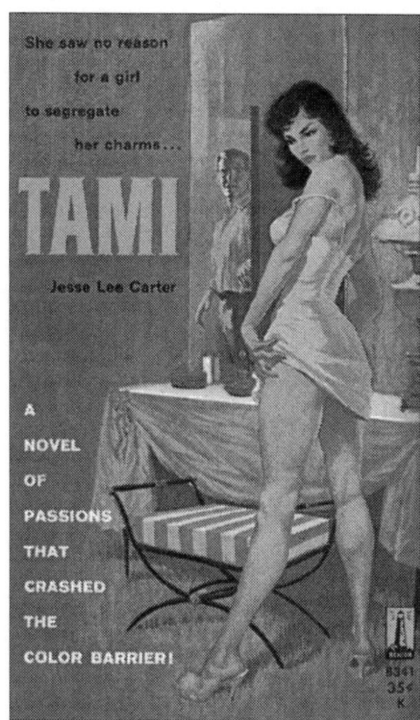

and wrote and produced a documentary for L.A. television station KNBC. He wrote for *Life* and *Ebony* magazines as well and conducted the first magazine interview with Black Muslim leader Elijah Muhammad, published in *Cavalier*.

In the 1960s, he went east to live on Long Island and became editor, bizarrely, of all things, the fan magazines *Hollywood Teen Album* and *Teen Stars Album*, published by Hanro. That was around the same time he wrote *Naked in Hollywood*; synergy in action. A gossip item in the March 1963 *Negro Digest* reported that his next book would be an interracial romance, *The Blacker the Berry*, and that he would follow that with his big novel at last, a study of interracial love in the suburbs tentatively titled *The Split-Level Plantation*. Sadly, I can't find any evidence that either of those books were ever published, even though a 1970 article also foretold the latter's release. That article revealed that his latest (last?) book was nonfiction, a study of boxer Jack Johnson titled *Black Gladiator*, meant to counteract the fictions told about Johnson in the movie *The Great White Hope*. He went back west to work for *Jet* and wrote no more books, with one possible exception. "Robert (Bob) Lucas & Ralph H. Chambers" copyrighted a book called *Down Tarrytown Road* in 1969, but again I can't find a trace of its physical existence.

Lucas had a wife named Millie, who must have predeceased him because she's not mentioned in his obituary. A son, Robert Lucas, Jr., a daughter, four grandchildren, and two great-grandchildren survived him.

He may have had only one story in him, but he was totally professional at telling and recasting it.

"Luke Roberts" has a relatively thoroughly documented life, but "Jesse Lee Carter" is as much a phantom as *The Split-Level Plantation*. No biographical information is forthcoming, nor a hint of another name. The only other book credited to him is *Tami*, Beacon B341, copyright 1960. The back cover blurb has a seeming quote, published in all-caps with red lettering:

> *. . . A COURAGEOUSLY OUTSPOKEN NOVEL, PROBING A HUSH-HUSH SIDE OF OUR SOCIETY NO PUBLISHER WOULD HAVE DARED TO EXPLORE TEN YEARS AGO.*

That's technically true, proving that you should never trust technical truths or back-cover blurbs. *Tami* is, of course, a reprinting of *Hot Chocolate*. Beacon was Arnold Abramson's mass-market sleaze line, the one that replaced his digest lines in 1954. *Tami* may or may not have been publishable in 1950, but his own company dared to publish it in 1952. Worse, Abramson's courage in 1960 is eminently doubtful. The girl on *Tami*'s cover may charitably be called tanned, but she has distinctly white features. Nowhere on the covers or the inside blurb is she referred to as nonwhite, either. For all we know she could have been "crossing the color line" with passions that "crashed the color barrier!" with a black lover.

Sleaze is in the eye of the beholder. It's the publishers who made damn sure that would-be readers got their proper eyeful.

Abramson's companies had plenty of flaws—low payments to authors, misleading covers and blurbs, books retitled to hide that they were reprints—but his releasing a line of paperbacks aimed at black readers, original novels at that, has to be commended for its courage. No other major paperback firm dared to do that in the 1950s. Bronze Books were utterly unique, desperately needed, and way ahead of their time.

Steve Carper's big fat book on the history of robots in popular culture is scheduled for 2019. "Outtakes" from the book can be found in a biweekly column on <Blackgate.com>. The site for all his future history is <FlyingCarsandFoodPills.com>. His digest novel collection has just hit 1100.

The Creature from the Black Lagoon with The Seven Year Itch

Article by Tom Brinkmann

"... then suddenly he turned on me, his eyes bulging, frothing at the mouth, just like the *Creature from the Black Lagoon*!"
–Marilyn Monroe as "The Girl" in *The Seven Year Itch* (1955)

This is an article I started in October 2017 which was to be on just *The Creature from the Black Lagoon* because I had the *Mechanix Illustrated* and *Science Fiction Digest* both with the *Creature* covers and the film, *The Shape of Water*, had just been released. Then a year later, when watching a DVD of *The Seven Year Itch* I noticed the marquee of the theatre playing the *Creature* movie. And, it grew from there with several other inputs along the way, namely the books *Room to Dream* by David Lynch and Kristine McKenna and *The Lady from the Black Lagoon* by Mallory O'Meara. So, my mind was tucked into some strange corners but, these two movies' tenuous relationship to each other because of the time (mid-1950s) and the use of the *Creature from the Black Lagoon* in *The Seven Year Itch* intrigued me.

The one story I really wanted to find, I couldn't—who was it that came up with the idea of featuring the *Creature* movie in the *Itch* movie, and why? Most likely George Axelrod, possibly Billy Wilder; they both could have known William Alland in Hollywood and knew of his wishes for his *Creature* movie to evoke empathy with the audience, hence, The Girl/Monroe's comments when leaving the show.

Origin of The Creature from the Black Lagoon

The conception of *Creature from the Black Lagoon* (1954) is a convoluted journey that apparently started at the home of Orson Welles (1915–1985) in 1941, who was having a dinner party with William Alland (1916–1997) who had met Welles in New York at the Henry Street Settlement House. Alland was an early member of Welles' Mercury Theatre repertory company started in 1937 in New York, and was a voice in Welles' infamous Halloween 1938 *Mercury Theatre On the Air*

Right: Marilyn Monroe, outside the Trans Luxe theatre with its marquee re-dressed for the *Creature from the Black Lagoon*, with Billy Wilder (black suit) and Tom Ewell (with cigarette). (Photographer unknown.)

Creature from the Black Lagoon 1954 Classic Monsters Ultimate Guide No. 8 2016
Above Leftt: Front Cover, Above Rightt: Back Cover

broadcast of *The War of the Worlds*; Alland had also been in *Citizen Kane* as the reporter "Thompson." Gabriel Figueroa (1907–1997), a Mexican cinematographer who was at the same dinner party, kept it lively by telling a tale of an Amazonian "fish-man," that the natives both feared and worshipped.

Alland made a mental note, and in October 1952, he wrote a short script to show Universal, titled *The Sea Monster* which had come to him from remembering Figueroa's "fish-man" story, heard over a decade earlier, at Welles' party. Universal thought it had potential and gave it to Leo Lieberman and Arthur Ross to whip into shape as a screenplay.

O'Meara wrote, "But the version of the screenplay that Ross and Lieberman had written still wasn't right. Alland wanted his *King Kong*-esque story. He wanted a movie with Beauty and the Beast elements."

The *Creature* was Universal-International's black and white 3-D film of a Lovecraftian creature, "Gill-Man" (Ben Chapman, did the land scenes and Ricou Browning the underwater scenes)," an amphibian/human combo, in a *Beauty and the Beast* scenario.

A book titled simply *Creature from the Black Lagoon* by Vargo Statten was published in England by Dragon Publications Limited in 1954. Vargo Statten was one of the many pseudonyms of John Russell Fearn (1908–1960), a British pulp writer. The original cover art was by John Richards.

In 1977, Berkley Medallion Books published a movie-tie-in paperback series called "Universal Horror Library," which contained volumes on *The Mummy*, *The Bride of Frankenstein*, *The Werewolf of London*, *Dracula's Daughter*, *The Wolfman*, and *Creature from the*

Black Lagoon, all written by "Carl Dreadstone" a pseudonym used by at least two people. *Creature from the Black Lagoon* by Carl Dreadstone had an introduction by Ramsey Campbell, but the book was written by Walter Harris, another UK writer and BBC radio personality. On the title-page it said, "Adapted from the screenplay by Arthur Ross and Harry Essex" and under that, also said, "From a story by Maurice Zimm." Zimm wrote the "original story treatment" for *Creature from the Black Lagoon*.

Forty years after Statten's book, "Amphibian Man," was a theme revisited more recently, explicitly, and erotically in Guillermo del Toro's, *The Shape of Water* (2017), which was set in Baltimore in 1962; the film won four Academy Awards. Daniel Kraus wrote the movie-tie-in novel *The Shape of Water* (2018), which is not related to the 1994 Italian book of the same name by Andrea Camillri.

Science Fiction Digest Vol. 1 No. 1 1954

Specific Fiction Corp.
145 West 57th Street
New York 19, NY
Editorial Offices: 341 Bleeker Street, New York, NY
162 pages, 35¢
5.25" x 7.25"

Science Fiction Digest's only two advertisements were on the back cover and both were from Authentic Publications, Inc. which, not surprisingly, was located at 145 West 57th Street in New York, at the same address as Specific Fiction Corporation. The ads were all text with no illustrations or photos for two books, "How to Adjust Your Television Set" (48 pages) and "Automobile Trouble-Shooter" (64 pages).

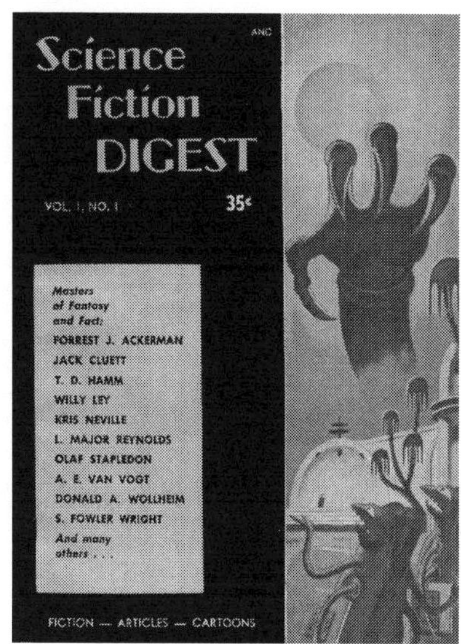

Science Fiction Digest No. 1 1954

Editor Chester Whitehorn (1923–1996) had also edited the only two issues of *Vortex* in 1953. Earlier in the mid-1940s he had written the essay "The Vizigrath" which was published in *Planet Stories* Winter 1945 and Summer 1946 issues.

Science Fiction Digest was quite diverse in its sources in picking of fiction and articles for its pages, in fact, here is a list of the articles and where they originated:

"Will Your Child Visit the Moon" by Jack Cluett from *Woman's Day*
"Interplanetary Man" by Olaf Stapledon from *Fate*
"Serendipity" by Joe Callanan from *The Lamp*
"Your Life In 1977!" by Willy Ley from *Man's Magazine*

And, some of its fiction:

"The Mitr" by Jack Vance from *Vortex*
"'Haunted Atoms'" by A.E. van Vogt from *Authentic Science Fiction*
"Dwellers in the Dust" by Forrest J. Ackerman from *Fantasy Book*
"Entrance Exam"

by E.C. Tubb from *New Worlds*
"Time Check for Control"
by Robert Sheckley from *Climax*
"Mimie" by Donald A. Wollheim
from *Astonishing Stories*

One of the "Special Features" was titled, "The World Is Changing: The Climate" by H. M. Mack, which is interesting for various reasons, but mainly because it was written in 1954 and sounds like it could have come from current talk radio, magazine articles, or the internet. It has become a cliché now, but Mack starts out by writing of his great-grandfather's stories about winter in New York City when he was a young boy in the nineteenth century. For instance:

> *My great-grandfather, a pioneer settler whose word nobody ever had cause to doubt, could remember having driven a carriage and pair across the ice-bound East River, a journey impossible in our time; my grandfather had equally vivid memories of the great blizzard of '88, another event that has not been duplicated for us; my own father assures me that the winters now are never so severe as when he was a boy, and complains that the summers in New York have become almost tropical—all of which leads to the conclusion that the climate has grown much warmer in the course of only three generations.*

It backed-up *The Seven Year Itch* with climate history facts! Monroe was living in tropical New York; the iconic skirt billowing scene was all a foreshadowing of climate change! So, in a way Marilyn Monroe's oracular cooter was talking to humanity in 1955, warning us of the coming climate crisis. Now it all makes sense, a prophetic warning from the Goddess.

Science Fiction Digest
Vol. 1 No. 2 1954

Specific Fiction Corp.
145 West 57th Street
New York 19, NY
162 pages, 35¢
5.25" x 7.25"

In the editorial titled "S.F.D. Notes" editor Whitehorn wrote about the changes in the digest since the first issue, mainly that it was going bi-monthly, starting to sell subscriptions, and getting into Hollywood to report on the new crop of sci-fi films.

Complete fiction in the issue:

"School Days" by James Causey
from *Science Stories*
"The Venus Gipsy"
by C. M. Webster from *Vortex*
"Miss Medford's Moon"
by Martin Gardner from *Esquire*
"The Evidence" by Sidney E. Porcelain
from *Off Trail Review*
"The Pine Branch"
by Claus Stamm from *Vague*
"Alphabet Scoop"
by Ross Rocklynn from *Nebula*
"Spacemen in the Dark"
by Robert Sheckley from *Climax*
"Part of My Past" by Richey McPherson
from *Neurotica*
"Man of the Hour"
by Robert Sheckley from *Impact*

The short two-page article that opened the issue was "A True Story" by Eartha Kitt (1927–2008) titled "My Experience with the Supernatural." Eartha Kitt (over a decade later, "Catwoman" on the *Batman* TV series) writes of reading tea leaves when a teenager as a goof, and then had a vision of "Johnny," the son of the family Kitt and her mother were living with at the time, running from a robbery down a dark "hall" or alley, with bundles of money, who then tripped over a barrel and is hit in the stomach by a police bullet. Years later, after Kitt had moved on, she was informed that what she had predicted as a teenager had come to pass just as she had seen it. Johnny had died fleeing a robbery and had been shot in the stomach. Creepy.

Editor Whitehorn attached "S. F. D. Introduces A New Department," to the end of the Kitt story. Whitehorn was soliciting personal stories from his readership on their experiences with the supernatural for his new department of which Kitt's article was the first.

"An S. F. D. Experiment" asked, "Are you clairvoyant?" and had five symbols, a triangle, an X, a circle, an asterisk, and an equal sign, and twenty-five numbered spaces were provided for the reader to fill in with symbols from the five given, using ESP/clairvoyance to predict what order they would be listed on another page in the issue.

Paramount producer George Pal (1908–1980) was asked to answer the question, "Has Hollywood Gone Science Fiction Mad?" as a request from *S. F. D.* i.e., editor Whitehorn. So, the feature of the same title was Pal's four-page answer. Pal chooses two films he produced, H. G. Wells', *The War of the Worlds* (1953) and, *Conquest of Space* (1955) for examples of science-fiction and science-fact, respectively.

After much discussion and defining, by Pal and others that he quotes from, about what constitutes Science-Fiction, Pal came to this conclusion:

> *If this comparatively new field is presented logically, in step-by-step fashion, avoiding the silly stories that are too improbable and fantastic even to be classed as fantasy, I think it will be only a matter of time before Hollywood goes "science-fiction mad." I suspect most movie fans, s-f experts or not, will be loving the mania.*

Science Fiction Digest No. 2 1954

Whitehorn wrote a short editorial comment that was placed in a box at the conclusion of the article, "Hypnotism and Ads vs. Me and Thee." The comment read:

> *I refuse as editor of Science Fiction Digest to cut, edit or digest the very guts of the material I publish. I don't like reading abridged writing, and I won't publish it. My dictionary accepts "digest" as a collection or summary, and I accept this for S. F. D.*

There were two *Creature* features in this issue, both went uncredited (probably written by Whitehorn), "Behind the Cover" and in the "S.F. Filmfare" section was "The Creature from the Black Lagoon—The Story," a synopsis of the film.

Movie Club No. 10 Spring 1997

"Behind the Cover" was a one-page article that gave some little-known facts about the "Gill-Man," such as four suits of his skin were "worn out before the film was completed." 132 scenes were filmed underwater, which translated into 32 days underwater for that segment of the crew; it was filmed on locations in Hollywood, Will Rodgers Beach in Santa Monica, California, and Wakulla Springs, Florida. Richard Carlson, Julia Adams, and Richard Denning went to an "underwater drama class," as the article went on to say, "In the studio's big tank on the back lot, the thespians rehearsed for almost a week to project drama strong enough to register for the camera from behind aqua-lung face masks."

It is interesting to compare this description of the Creature's creation given here with the one given in *Mechanix Illustrated* below:

> *Months of research, experimentation and tests were spent before the monstrous Gill-Man came to life. Make-up chief Bud Westmore and his assistant, Jack Kevan, analyzed 25 volumes devoted to strange creatures of the deep, prehistoric mammals and artists' conceptions of fictional monsters. A total of 76 sketches of the body and 32 of the head were submitted, and almost 200 pounds of rubber and plastic went into life-sized models of the monster's body before the choice was made.*

This second issue moved the two ads from the first issue inside and put a third ad from Authentic Publications, Inc., on the back cover, this one a booklet for "120 House Models Attractive and Practical," "A House for Every Budget."

Mechanix Illustrated: The How-To-Do Magazine Vol. 50 No. 5 May 1954

Fawcett Publications, Inc.
67 West 44th Street
New York 36, NY
228 pages, 20¢
6.5″ x 9.25″

Mechanix Illustrated was launched in 1928 as competition for *Popular Mechanics* which had been around since 1902. Wikipedia says of *Mechanix Illustrated*, ". . . it went through a number of permutations over the years, being called at various points in its life, *Modern Mechanics and Inventions*, *Modern Mechanix and Inventions*, *Modern Mechanix*, *Mechanix Illustrated*, *Home Mechanix*, and, in its final incarnation, *Today's Homeowner*." It stopped publication with the March/April 2001 issue.

The cover story on this May 1954 issue, "Science Creates a Monster" by Harvey B. Jones started with the blurb, "Hollywood has produced some weird costumes, but this $18,000 horror-suit tops them all." The piece contained seven black and white photos; the largest being of the Creature holding a swooning Julie Adams in his arms, titled "The Triumphant Gill-Man"; three pics of the special effects crew working on the costume, including one of Bud Westmore and Chris Mueller "putting final touches to rear section of the monster costume"; one pic of the crew filming underwater; and two pics of Ben Chapman as the Creature swimming underwater.

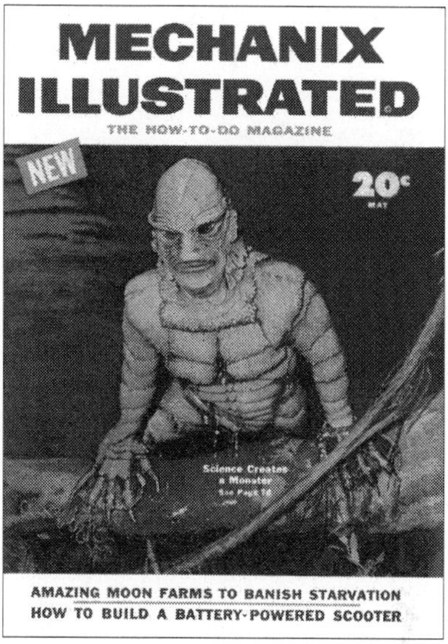

To his credit, Jones gave Milicent Patrick credit, and wrote:

> *Original designs for the weird costume were drawn by Milicent Patrick, a statuesque Hollywood beauty who is both artist and actress rolled into one. After working for a while for Walt Disney as the first girl animator in history, she was hired to create monsters for Bud Westmore at Universal-International. Some of her horrifying handiwork has appeared in* It Came from Outer Space, This Island Earth *and* Sign of The Pagan. *The Gill-Man is her masterpiece, however. She had to change his shape 76 times before he finally was approved and now, no matter how he scares people, she still thinks he's cute.*

And continued:

> *But actual designs were just the first step. Once Bud Westmore and Jack Kevan, the well-known make-up artist, got hold of the sketches it was their problem to actually create the monster. In the first place, the costume had to be completely waterproof since most of the action involving the Gill-Man would take place under water.*

The cover on this May 1954 issue of *Mechanix Illustrated* was the first appearance of the *Creature* on a cover. And, the second was on *The Skin Diver* August 1954 (Vol. 3 No. 8).

It went on to explain all the difficulties they had to make the suit usable underwater while at the same time Ben Chapman had to be able to swim in it convincingly. Each segment of his body was cast with plaster and turned into rubber and it all had to fit together seamlessly to be watertight. The most amazing fact was that the hands and feet, "had to be made with special controls so that they would actually aid Chapman in his underwater swimming instead of weighing him down." And, they went through 32 head models before choosing the one that was used.

Note: This article mentions that Ben Chapman was doing the swimming, everywhere else credited Ricou Browning as doing the underwater Creature but Browning was not mentioned in this article.

At the end of the article it gave the story that Julie Adams, had in fact been knocked unconscious from her head hitting a rock when the Creature took a sharp turn bringing her to his cave-lair, her injury was not noticed until after the scene was shot. When the crew did notice, she was brought to the studio hospital, "where she was treated for a minor concussion and skin abrasions. She recovered in a few days . . ."

At the end, Jones boiled it down by stating, "It's an underwater 3-D Frankenstein." Ultimately, it was a success by 1950s monster movie standards and spawned two other films, *Revenge of the Creature* (1955) and, *The Creature Walks Among Us* (1956) in my opinion the first is a classic, the second useless, and the third was possibly the best.

Enter "The Lady from the Black Lagoon"

When Milicent Patrick, born: Mildred Elizabeth Fulvia di Rossi (1915–1998) first met Bud Westmore, born: Hamilton Adolph Westmore (1918–1973) in 1952, she was 37 years old, had worked as an animator for Disney, and acted in movies. When she showed Westmore some of her drawings, he knew he had just found someone with talent, and hired her for his make-up/special effects department at Universal-International.

Bud Westmore—the name conjures up the magazine *Famous Monsters of Filmland* for me; he was supposed to be a monster make-up wizard. Westmore came from a Hollywood make-up dynasty, "The Westmores," which had been started by his father, Bud was apparently an ego maniac and took most of the spotlight and credit for work that his team of artists, both make-up and special effects people, created. His nasty disposition came to the fore with Milicent Patrick, "The Lady from the Black Lagoon," and the way in which he and Universal-International treated her, by firing her for doing her job well, maybe too well.

In fact, Universal decided to send Patrick on a two-week—which turned into a month-long—publicity tour promoting the *Creature* movie and the other Universal monsters, which she agreed to. The tour kicked off in New York City on February 1, 1954 with television and radio interviews, as well as print journalists. At first, the tour was dubbed "The Beauty Who Created the Beast," but because Westmore wanted all the credit, was quickly changed to, "The Beauty Who Lives with the Beasts."

On February 12, 1954 the movie premiered in Detroit to a good reception; both Milicent Patrick and the film's only female, Julie Adams, were there together; its general release date was March 5th. The tour, in which Milicent Patrick traveled the country and had done forty interviews on radio, television, newspapers, and magazines. Patrick was not under contract to Universal but a freelance artist that Westmore had promised she could come back to her job and pick up where she had left off, which was working on *This Island Earth*. The problem was Westmore had been monitoring Patrick's tour and interviews from California and was furious that he was not mentioned as much in the interviews as he thought he should have been and decided to fire her when she got back. And, he did.

O'Meara writes in her book:

Right away, the guys on Universal's publicity team knew what was really going on. They were the people that Bud complained about Milicent to, so when the news spread, they knew what had happened and why. They knew it wasn't Milicent's fault. They knew the blame lay squarely on Bud Westmore's inflamed ego.

Despite all efforts to reverse Westmore's decision, he would not budge and Universal went with it. So, when she got back from her successful tour, she also got the news of her dismissal from Universal. Patrick was devastated at finding herself unemployed when she got back, but being dignified, she didn't give Westmore or Universal any push-back, she just went on with her life.

The Seven Year Itch Bantam Books No. 1371, 1955

The Seven Year Iitch

Easily my favorite Marilyn Monroe film, the 20th Century-Fox film *The Seven Year Itch* (1955) starred Monroe as "The Girl" and Tom Ewell as "Richard Sherman," a married man in New York City whose wife and child are out of town for the summer in Ogunquit, Maine. It started out as a romantic comedy play by George Axelrod (1922–2003) which premiered at the Fulton Theatre in New York on November 20, 1952 which also starred Tom Ewell, with Vanessa Brown, the first actress to play "The Girl." Billy Wilder (1906–2002) worked on the screenplay with Axelrod.

Their biggest nemesis was the Hays Code, the Production Code for movies which caused them to have to rewrite the stage play to suit the screen, and because the Girl and Richard Sherman did have sex in the stage version. When they got done with the rewrite Sherman was just fantasizing, and a lot of the racy jokes and situations came out as adultery was not a fit subject for comedy. Wilder said he wished he'd waited to the 1970s to make to make it after the Motion Picture Association of America (MPAA) rating system was put in place November 1, 1968. But of course, if he had, he wouldn't have had Marilyn Monroe in it, which would have made it moot.

The Creature from the Black Lagoon also had its problems with the Hays Code; mainly they wanted Universal to assure them there would be no bestiality, insinuated or otherwise, between the Creature and Kay (Julie Adams). Universal assured them there wouldn't be.

Tom Ewell reading *U.S. Camera Annual* 1952, while Vanessa Brown looks on in the stage production of *The Seven Year Itch.*

The saying "the seven-year itch" comes from a fictitious book that was quoted from in the movie as "Richard Sherman" was an editor at a paperback publisher that is planning to publish *Man and the Unconscious* by Dr. Ludwig Brubaker. One of the chapters of which was titled, "The Repressed Urge of the Middle-Aged Male: Its Roots and Consequences."

It seems, to my perverse mind, that the sub-plot of the film was to keep "The Girl's" aka Monroe's cooter as cool as possible, as much of the time as possible. Her real itch in the film came from the ninety-five-degree summer heat of New York City. When she first enters the film, and apartment building, she is carrying a bag of groceries, that included a wax paper bag of Bell potato chips whose manufacturer had sent cartons of them to the set; and a small plug-in fan whose plug is dragging behind her so that it gets caught in the door for the fan/fanny joke, as she ascends the stairs in a super tight dress that emphasized her "fanny." So, her saving grace came from her iced "undies," fans, air conditioning, and subway grates, breezes all aimed up her skirt.

On September 15, 1954, Marilyn Monroe proceeded to catch her "delicious," up-lifting, and historic breeze, on Lexington Avenue. As a publicity stunt, thanks to a New York newspaper, hundreds of photographers and male gawkers showed up at two a.m., including Monroe's husband Joe DiMaggio and his friend Walter Winchell, to catch a glimpse of Monroe on a subway grate. A cooling breeze was just what she needed after getting all worked-up over seeing the film *Creature from the Black Lagoon* (1954), Monroe quipped:

The Girl (Monroe): *Didn't you just love the picture? I did. But I just felt so sorry for the creature, at the end.*

Richard Sherman (Ewell): *Sorry for the creature? What'd you want him to marry the girl?*

The Girl: *He was kind of scary looking, but he wasn't really all bad. I think he just craved a little affection you know, a sense of being loved, and needed, and wanted.*

Richard Sherman: *That's a very interesting point of view*

There was a line that Monroe delivered in the scene that was cut out to please the Hays Code; after the second train went by and blows her skirt up once more, she commented, "This one's even cooler! Must have been an express! Don't you wish you had a skirt? I feel so sorry for you in those hot pants."

George Axelrod, the screenwriter said of Monroe in a 1972 interview: "I knew her genuine, almost child-like, passion for pets and animals. I knew that she would identify, not with victims of the *Creature from the Black Lagoon*, but with the *Creature from the Black Lagoon* itself."

That statement is interesting considering information given in O'Meara's book that Universal gave the script to Maurice Zimm who wrote a wacky version that ended with the Creature being eaten by piranhas, "but it gave Alland the kind of monster that he really wanted. He wanted a dignified creature full of humanity, something that was barely monstrous."

The location of the shoot was 590 Lexington Avenue at 52nd Street, in front of the Henry Steig jewelry store. Henry Steig (1906–1973) was an interesting guy (Google him) and had recently moved to that location from his first location at 51st Street and First Avenue.

The dress Monroe wore for the scene was designed by William Travilla (1920–1990) who commented on his design, saying:

> *I wanted her to look fresh and clean. So I wondered what could I do with this most beautiful girl . . . to make her look talcum-powdered and adorable. What would I give her to wear that would blow in the breeze and be fun and pretty? I knew there would be a wind blowing so that would require a skirt.*

Debbie Reynolds, a collector of Hollywood memorabilia, retrieved the dress from the Twentieth Century-Fox wardrobe department where it had been since the 1950s and auctioned it off for 5.6 million dollars on June 18, 2011. Reynolds reportedly was in tears at the auction's end, having thought it would only command two million dollars.

The theatre, shown in the background, that Monroe and Ewell had just left as they walked down Lexington Ave., was not running *Creature from the Black Lagoon*, as a quote from Roy Craft, someone who was there as part of the crew, explained:

> *The production crew had picked this Lexington Avenue newsreel theatre* [the Trans Luxe], *which they had in those days—the crew had picked this one because at two in the morning the street is entirely deserted and we'd have no problem. So they re-dressed the theatre with this monster movie and so forth.*

When they reshot the scene on a set in Hollywood, special effects man Paul Wurtzel, was called upon to provide the subway breeze that delighted Monroe, and that also delighted Wurtzel who got a unique view of that scene. Wurtzel remembered:

> *We went on all day. I do recall (that) Marilyn, when she was lined up for the shot, she'd squat down and there I'd be, looking up at Marilyn and you know, we'd be talking to one another—"How's everything going?" and "Too bad you have to do the scene over and over again"—we were a good six hours until Billy Wilder got what he wanted.*

Wurtzel concluded by saying, "Not realizing what the later publicity would be from it, I thought it was just another assignment—a hell of a nice assignment. The only thing I got out of it (then) was a cinder

U.S. Camera July 1955 with Tom Ewell reading *U.S. Camera 20th Anniversary Edition 1955*

fell in my eye, but we got that out eventually . . ." A moral to the story?

In 1999, Billy Wilder revealed in an interview, "I had guys fighting as to who was going to put the ventilator on, in the shaft there, below the grill."

The scene was *not* a hit with DiMaggio who stormed off on foot back to the St. Regis Hotel where they were staying, when Monroe returned from the shoot, DiMaggio reportedly beat her, which effectively ended their marriage. He had been deeply embarrassed by his wife's public behavior.

There were several magazines that ran Monroe's famous skirt blowing pics from *The Seven Year Itch* on their covers at the time, *Se* (October 7, 1954) a Swedish photojournalism mag, *Police Gazette* (February 1955) and *Man to Man* (May 1955); the Italian magazine *Visioni* also ran it on the cover of their May 14, 1955 issue. *Movie Stars Parade* (September 1955) used Monroe's skirt blowing pics as a duo-tone background with her in color in the foreground. The iconic photo could also be found on the inside of many movie and girlie magazines from the mid-50s on. It was brilliant advertising using the sub-plot of the "delicious breeze," as was the 52-foot cut-out banner of Monroe with skirt billowing out above Loew's State Theatre in Times Square, which was taken down not long after it was put up, because of complaints.

The Seven Year Itch premiered on June 1, 1955, Monroe's 29th birthday, she attended with her husband Joe DiMaggio, almost divorced but, not yet, the divorce was finalized on Halloween 1955.

U.S. Camera
Vol. 18 No. 7 July 1955

U.S. Camera Publishing Corp.
420 Lexington Ave.
New York 17, NY
118 pages, 35¢
8.5″x 11″

The address of U.S. Camera Publishing was 420 Lexington Avenue, just down the street, so-to-speak, from where Monroe's skirt blowing scene was filmed. *U.S. Camera* premiered in 1935 as an annual book, at first spiral bound, eventually as hardcover volumes with dust jackets. The magazine *U.S. Camera* started in 1938, and Marilyn Monroe was not a newcomer to *U.S. Camera*'s readers in 1955, as she had been one of three women photgraphed by Andre De Dienes on the cover of the November 1944 issue , which was Monroe's first magazine cover, and one of four young ladies featured on the May 1946 issue, again by De Dienes; and a 1962 George Barris headshot of Monroe was featured on the cover of

U.S. Camera 20th Anniversary Edition 1955

Here is one of the scenes from the forthcoming film in which *U.S. Camera* plays an important role.

U.S. Camera Annual 1964 edition.

U.S. Camera Annual 1952 was used in the stage version of *The Seven Year Itch*. A curious thing in the film *The Seven Year Itch* is that the photo shown, of a young Monroe laying on her stomach, on a beach in a red and white striped bikini; the title of the photo in the film was "Three Textures," as The Girl/Monroe explained, one texture was the driftwood, another the sand, and she was the third texture. The photo shown in the film was most likely taken by Laszlo Willinger in 1947, but it was not in the *U.S. Camera 20th Anniversary Edition 1955* shown in the film. I searched the Internet and my multifarious books on Marilyn Monroe and could not find it anywhere. What is on page 114, is a black and white head shot of Monroe by famed photographer Andre De Dienes. The caption read, "This head shot was made in a Beverly Hills driveway at midnight, lit by car headlights." It is a wistful and melancholy portrait of Monroe not often seen.

"*U.S. Camera Annual* Stars in '*Seven Year Itch*'" was a three-page feature that included nine black and white photos, three of which were behind-the-scene pics with lights, cameras and crew in them. In the lead splash-page photo, Monroe clutches an open copy of *U.S. Camera Annual* to her bosom, with the caption, "Here is one of the scenes from the forthcoming film in which *U.S. Camera Annual* plays an important role."

The text in this article seems to wink at the reader using quotation marks and italics, winking because they knew there were no nudes of Monroe in *U. S. Camera*, saying, "[Sherman/Ewell] meeting with the girl (Marilyn Monroe) from the apartment upstairs and the 'nude' photograph of her in *U. S. Camera Annual* make for an hilarious comedy."

And, "When the girl upstairs

visits him and discovers he has a copy of the *Annual*, she informs him of her past as a model and shows him the picture in the book of her . . . *in the nude*."

They even showed the page in question in the movie, and it was not a nude, and as mentioned above, the page shown in the film was not in that issue of *U. S. Camera Annual*.

Afterword

In 1986 writer Mark Frost was working in Los Angeles for United Artists on a film adaptation of the biography *Goddess: The Secret Lives of Marilyn Monroe* by Anthony Summers. This is when fate played its hand and he met David Lynch. Fate took the form of an agent from the Creative Artists Agency (CAA) who had introduced the two. Frost and Lynch worked well together but United Artists got cold feet when they read the script, titled *Venus Descending*, and when they realized that Bobby Kennedy had been "implicated" in Monroe's death, the film was scrapped. Lynch and Frost of course went on to create the ground breaking television series *Twin Peaks* for ABC in 1990 and have collaborated on *Twin Peaks: Fire Walk with Me* (1992), *On the Air* (1992) a seven-episode television series for ABC, and *Twin Peaks: The Return* (2017).

> *Marilyn Monroe was this loose cannon there* [Kennedy's Camelot] *at the end and they had to get rid of her. But it's a story I kept loving. You could say that Laura Palmer is Marilyn Monroe, and that* Mulholland Drive *is about Marilyn Monroe, too. Everything is about Marilyn Monroe.*

–David Lynch from *Room to Dream* 2018

Tom Brinkmann writes about unusual off-the-beaten-path magazines, digests, and tabloids. His book *Bad Mags* was published in two volumes in 2008/09. Anyone seriously interested in purchasing his *Bad Mags* archive/collection can contact him at: <vaioduct@aol.com>

REFERENCES

Axelrod, George, "The Complete Play *The Seven Year Itch*," and "A Hit In A Hurry" *Theatre Arts* Vol. 38 No. 1 January 1954.

Axelrod, George, *The Seven Year Itch: A Romantic Comedy* New York: Bantam Books, 1955.

Burton, Nige and Jamie Jones, *Creature from the Black Lagoon 1954 Classic Monsters Ultimate Guide* No. 8. London: UK, 2016.

Crown, Lawrence, *Marilyn at Twentieth Century Fox* London: Comet Books, 1987.

Kidder, Clark, *Marilyn Monroe Cover to Cover* (1st and 2nd editions). Wisconsin: Krause Publications, 1999.

Lynch, David and Kristine McKenna, *Room to Dream* New York: Random House, 2018.

Maloney, Tom (ed.), *U. S. Camera 20th Anniversary Edition 1955* New York: U. S. Camera Publishing Corp., 1954.

Nickens, Christopher and George Zeno, *Marilyn In Fashion: The Enduring Influence of Marilyn Monroe* Philadelphia: Running Press Book Publishers, 2012.

O'Meara, Mallory, *The Lady from the Black Lagoon: Hollywood Monsters and the Lost Legacy of Milicent Patrick* Toronto: Hanover Square Press, 2019.

Thompson, Jeff, "The Creature's Features." *Movie Club* No. 10, Spring 1997.

Acknowledgement

Kathleen Banks Nutter, line editing.

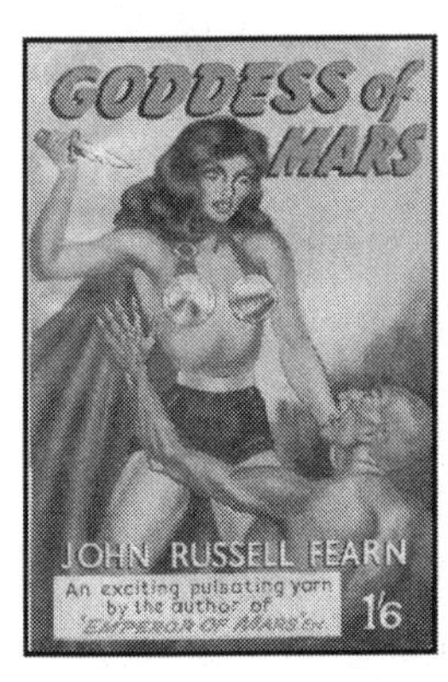
GODDESS of MARS
JOHN RUSSELL FEARN
An exciting pulsating yarn by the author of 'EMPEROR OF MARS'
1/6

35¢
REFORM SCHOOL GIRL
FELICE SWADOS

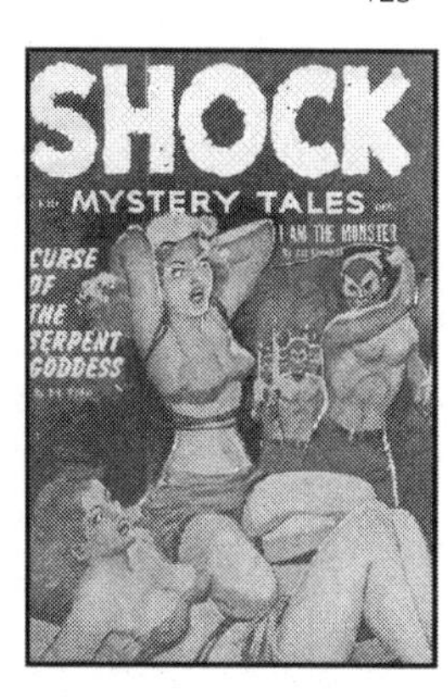
SHOCK
MYSTERY TALES
CURSE OF THE SERPENT GODDESS
I AM THE MONSTER

MANHUNT
DETECTIVE STORY MONTHLY
Mickey Spillane
EVERY STORY NEW!
JOHN ROSS MACDONALD
RICHARD S. PRATHER
DAVID GOODIS
RICHARD DEMING

SATURN
SCIENCE FICTION AND FANTASY
OCT.
CALIFORNIA IS DOOMED!

REAL Police Story MAGAZINE
25 Cents
RED OGRE of the DANUBE
ORIENTAL VENGEANCE

G Cruise

Fantasy fiction by Robert Snashall
Photo by Pexels from Pixabay

THE SEA MIST was thick, sticky, hot. Slicing through the humidity, a black hulk stalked the shoreline. At the head of the bay, the vessel pivoted 45 degrees bow forward and crept in. Compressing waves it hovered aiming at the port.

Gulls darted inland. The surf retreated. The shore patrol saw nothing on the water but floating seaweed. The signs were unmistakable. The locals had only a few moments.

"*Madre de Dios*, I'm not through taking the 'China' stickers off the turtle necklaces!" Louie de Paz griped under a "Make Winos Grape Again" ball cap. The tchotchke vendors had just enough time to stuff their heads with super high THC melting ear corks. But a mongoose now dancing in the cemetery had seized Louie's stash.

Then the wave struck.
And it wasn't water.

"Mermaid in Heels Stuck In the Sand Whoomp / Went to the Prom with a Surfing Band"

"*Arrrrgh los Gringos locos!*" Louie crumpled. A wave of sound hit the beach blasting a karaoke remix of retro rock.

The island news stringer duly filed her radio story of the rocking toxic tide once again striking the island community. The last thing they heard was the sign off, "Rock On!" Then nothing, all was still. Dead still.

". . . ALL WAS STILL—dead still." The radio station followed the news with rasta rap grabbing the cabbie's attention that Chauncey and Judy Hemptuffet in get-me-to-the-ship-on-time mode could ill afford to lose.

"Cabbie," rasped Chauncey through his inhaler, "can you please turn that racket off! We must get to the port to catch the cruise for the morning sailing!"

"Yesssuh mistah," the cabbie complied. The speedometer needle skyrocketed, the cab zooming around palmed roundabouts, lifting

off freeway runways, pell-melling due east for the shore. As it was it would be touch and go. They could spot the port terminal as they entered the last underpass just as a hayseed pizza delivery truck was swerving into the tunnel from the opposite direction. Judy squeezing his arm blue, Chauncey caught the truck lights flickering from neglected maintenance careening into their lane. They closed their eyes winging prayers. *Wa-Wap*! The vehicular Hail Mary passed by in a flash.

The cab sped on to the port, jettisoning Chauncey and Judy who were feeling no pain from the release. They made it! Not even the uncouth incivility of a rotund swamp cracker, who wouldn't hold the door open for Judy as she adjusted her shoe torturing her plantar fasciitis, dampened their spirits. Bags on the wheel they were specially ushered into a processing passageway guided by a spotless white uniformed porter who had waited for them holding a metallic sign with their names inscribed in gilt Saxon script.

"God, the Company thinks of everything," beamed Chauncey, "what a send-off!"

THE SCHEDULE FOR the afternoon shore excursion was civilized, allowing for wilting hearties to siesta on the good cruise ship Rottendam before venturing forth. But that was the problem.

While relishing a sound snooze as much as the next guy, Chauncey did not want to be part of the Nap Set. The co-cruisers on their corridor waddled, wheezed and weighted as addled members of Big Pharma's target audience. Their menus consisted entirely of scrimpy senior portions delivered a la tepid with plastic toothpicks to probe gelatin for stray shards of fruit cocktail. Chauncey was keen to scout for ship snacks. Alas, his attempt to walk around the deck was aborted by a bone spur and a locked steel door signed "Down the hatch. Cheers!"

"We can't go starboard," he lamented, "we're stuck in port."

"Snort?" Judy gushed,
"Oh Chaunce, let's do some
edibles to throttle the pain!
Will it be caramel or chocolate?"

"Make it a double."

Drifting up, Chauncey relished the prospect of the mandatory afternoon excursion. It no doubt included the safety evacuation drill to make sure passengers knew how to bail. Besides what a rush! After a tender ride to land, it promised to retrace the route of the conquistadores bushwhacking their way in their lust for gold and good libations. Just bring a swimsuit. But there was Judy to consider.

She wasn't quite on board with the endeavor. She was miffed jerks on that other passing cruise ship had totally ignored her waving. Plus, she had to do knee exercises and floss first.

Despite creeping alcohol sensitivity, Chauncey lured Judy with visions of the gin and tonics that were to be their reward for surviving the outing. They found themselves in line to board the tender bobbing up and down shipside across a plank. No sooner had they achieved the repose of knowing they hadn't screwed up the morning's myriad mundane hurdles of existence than a rumbling kerfuffle behind them upset the cue of the shuffling disheveled:

"Shit!"

A walker had escaped Suzi Burbol's grasp disrupting Chauncey in mid yawn. The hubbub caused Chauncey to spread his stiffening legs through which Suzi's SO Sy torpedoed in a diving catch to seize the metal walker fleeing for whatever sanity resides in titanium. And just so, as it was snatched at the point of tipping over the plank into the Big Drink.

Shot up before Chauncey's belt line was the free flailing hand that was somehow attached to Sy Burbol's balding dome sticking out under Chauncey's crotch. Chauncey got the message and shook it.

"I'm Chauncey Hemptuffet and that's Judy, behind you."

"Sy Burbol here, and Suzi is the swinging gimpette."

"Pleasure."

Sy didn't miss a beat. "We're from Brooklyn. Flew down in a storm. If you can grab the walker, I'll pull out. Deal?"

"OK."

The walker rescued per Chauncey, Sy was as good as his word. With a grunt Sy hefted himself up on one scarred knee then boosted up straightening out midriff flab scratching all the while. "For what I did to deserve this chronic rash I dunno.

Another interesting cruise day though, course it goes along with the story."

"Story?" Chauncey cast a brow up setting off an ocular tic.

"That phantom tidal tale on cruise channel 3 news. You must have heard it. No?"

"No.

"Yeah—no radio contact, no sightings, nothing.

"What?"

"Yeah, well there was something. It appears – strike that. It doesn't appear—"

"What?"

"Mish-mashed moldie oldies blare onto land. Drives the islanders bonkers especially the young rappers who can hear. Comes from who knows what and then it's gone."

"Gone?"

"Yeah, some kinda ghostly Terror of the Spanish Main shtick."

FROM AFAR THE pyramid was impressive. Four stories high, it presented a perfect photo op. Had the Mayans advanced this far? Or, maybe it was the work of some wayward ex-pat with time and a temperament on his hands, a paean to tropic life created by artistic license masquerading as romantic sensibility. You never knew what sort of exotica would pop up in the Spanish Main. Then they went ashore.

Judy, bladder calling, made a beeline for the banyo. Chauncey abided Gazing down at his fingers he yelped, "Yipes!" Reflexively, he buried his fingers into his underarms. He squirmed, fingers scraping pits. The horror of it! His fingernails had grown twistedly long, gnarling at the ends like fishing hooks.

"Too much shellfish protein—" Chauncey flashed as he retracted his claws snagging his polo shirt.

"Ooo that *smell*!" The remark interrupted Chauncey's withdrawal. It came from a super buff guy in the line-up of the otherwise doddering cruisers waiting on—who was it? Oh yes, their mates. Had a banyo bomb of poorly digested carbs detonated? No, it was more like the rank sweet odor of rot. "It's making me gag, I'm

Tony," he preened, "my body resents the retching, makes it hard to take a shit. Reminds me of the old days."

Chauncey was curious as this peacock was definitely a physical specimen, a species he had yet to encounter on the ship. "Smell?"

"Yo, terrible."

Chauncey was worried. He couldn't smell a thing. Good Gawd! Was it Old Man Time casting another joy into the oblivion of sensory deprivation? He'd have to play along.

"Smell."

"Yo." Tony eyed the line-up of the belching, quivering and crutched. "You guys look like you could use a drink! Phew, gross."

"Must be the pyramid," Chauncey offered.

"The pyramid?"

"Yo dude," Chaunceysplained, "it's that gigantic mound of garbage over there from the last storm."

JUDY EMERGED FROM the banyo, bedraggled, her hand wringing soapy drool. "There were no towels," she cried, "so I had to use an ass gasket."

Crisis called. Judy was not happy. The antidote? Adventure! Chauncey made another plug.

"Hey Jude—the excursion leaves right here from the pier in five so we'll soon be off in search of El Dorado."

"Coronado? I really like the Del—such a classy hotel—I wanna be loved by their martinis!"

"No not Coronado dear, Dorado, El Dorado. The fabled city of gold."

"Gold?" She lit. It was working.

"Five star reviews," he schmoosed locating her hand atrophying beneath the clinging humid shreds of tissue. "After a short bus ride, they're going to take us into the interior, a real foot safari tracing the path of Ponce de Leon!"

"Oh, I don't know. I'm not wearing the right shoes."

"It's only for a few hours. Pretty flat. Midway there'll be drinks and vendors before returning to our G and Ts shipshape!"

"Vendors?"

"I bet they're selling that deep pit amber."

"Amber?"

"We could get a good chunk with insects thrown in at a bargain."

"Bargain?"

He hooked her.

"And we can go back home to the old hippy jeweler in the houseboat when he shows up to work for a custom setting."

"In gold!"

"Yes. Perfect." It was looking up for the adventure. To live on the edge. A life spike!

But then it appeared. The brow scowl scrunched her face.

"Oh Chaunce, I don't know," her lower lip shot out as she picked at tissue shreds slithering over her gnarling fingers chipping the salon nail job. "I really prefer silver. Gold doesn't go with my coloring"—which Chauncey noticed was going off.

Sy Burbol stepped up to the plate to pinch hit. "Suzi and yours truly are going in! She's taking the walker and I've got anti-itch cream by the volume. I hear the drinks are good. And it's mandatory already. You pull out now, travel insurance won't cover your losses."

With such logic who can argue?

"YOU DIDN'T TELL me we would be strapped into a Humvee straddling trench sides at 90 degrees!" Uh oh—Judy's knack to pinpoint the obvious.

"Hey Jude this bus is part of the gig. As the Lama says, 'Live in the moment!'" Chauncey, the long of tooth Labrador pup, studiously ignored he was in her cross hairs.

"I'm bracing with my knee up against the roll bar!" She roared.

Eiyiyi! The Knee—her arthritic knee! Chauncey had to talk fast, which was a trick as his bicuspids, loosened from his abandoning the renegade water pick dousing the bathroom, were now in a spiral rattle. "Well Ju Ju Jude this issaisssss—"

"Get off it Chauncey! Cut the limp snake bit!"

While he had always entertained, at least himself, with his routines mimicking the beasts from Kipling's *Jungle Book*, now was not the time to stand on pride.

"Just the jiggling Jude. Here—" He doffed his outfitter's river hat with snap up brim and jammed it between her knee and the roll bar. "Cushioning accomplished!" Or so he thought without reckoning on thermodynamics as any energy from aborted impact transmogrified into a swipe of her curling talons across his exposed cranium blindingly reflecting the glint of the sun smoking his last few follicles. Poof! Their ashes ascended at the last lurch.

"ALL RIGHT *AMIGOS, arriba arriba*, let's go!" Out from the humbus sprung Algato Orlando, with rippling upper torso muscles, a powerful jaw line and flashy teeth honed to points—overall a tour guide version of the hard body that comes to clean the pool when you don't have one. He flung down a packed cooler of bottled water minis.

Suzi Burbol sat, humveed into immobilization. Sy, such a prince, jumped at being the therapist his mother always wanted. Looping around each middle finger and down on the palms he put on hand buzzers and applied to each of Suzi's temples. Zzzap! Shock therapy, effective and cheap, what was not to like? She jolted up. Sy had it down. Suzi and the walker exited as Sy with piercing fingernails got one more good scratch in.

"*Andale andale*!" Algato greeted each disembarking female jangle of bones with a mini bottle containing a shot of water. "Here *amiga*—have a taste of the journey. *Salud*!"

Suzi and Judy drank to the last drop, which was about all there was. "Get a load of that tush," they cackled snatching another round of bottled agua shots from the servicing hunk.

Algato postured himself between two palm fronds, machete resting firmly across his chiseled midsection. "Ready?"

Sy, stroking his paunch while ruminating a shift from stocks to bonds, adjusted Suzi's walker. Chauncey compared his shriveling legs to Algato's steel calves. Judy grasped a brittle clump of her hair holding it up to her crossing eyes. Geez—it was colored too red ruining the sienna-platinum bands of her 'do!

"*Bueno*!" Algato with a commanding sweep of a bicep parted the fronds exposing a trailhead with just enough overgrowth to signal adventure. "Single file. Stay close to me!"

Giggles.

The game was afoot.

HOW FAR HAD they gone? It was hard to say. They shambled through interminable bush skirting swamps. By a massive mangrove root, Suzi gulped her second water shot and heaved her walker into the brown ooze. "That thing was slowing me down!"

"Ah necessity," Sy shrugged, "the mother of feats."

They cut through hammocks of tropical growth snaking on tribal trails.

"Can't you just feel the natives hunting for . . . ?" Chauncey choked.

"Us," grunted Judy.

"Judy," Chauncey preached, "it's history."

"History shmystery!" She pointed low, "These sandals . . ."

His throat tightened. Beaded salt burned his eyes. And then the dreaded—

"*Blister*!" She bellowed.

"Moleskin at the ready!" Chauncey took her foot hard and reddened by settling blood. The blister bulged, it was the toughest he'd ever seen.

"I'm in survival mode. I need a drink!" No sooner had she swigged Algato's second serving then she stomped off, full weight on the blister. "Plantar be damned!"

"It's a wonder," said Sy, "what survival can achieve. There they are Judy and Suzi leading the column . . . with Algato."

As the women steamed on, the guys straggled, vigor evaporating. Sy rolled up like a hedgehog in a tax trance, calculating how to get around deduction caps. Chauncey drifted into a mirage. He saw himself, a sun crazed legionnaire, manfully braving the dunes. Until his balance gave out into Sy's backside caving in. Chauncey went down, bruising a blotchy purple like an ink smear run amuck. But, thank God, the cell phone was spared! Then he saw what stopped the column in its tracks – green and metallic, it wasn't vegetation. It was a sign, a huge sign—for the Conquistador Outlet Mall.

"Deals!" Judy and Suzi squealed.

"Now, now," Algato grinned, "we must go on *mi compadritas*! There will be mall time on the return leg." Lunging he clutched the females, "To the ancient treasure!"

The tropical temperature soared. Judy and Suzi had to agree, "Oooo Algato, it's history."

THE DECREPIT RECEPTACLES of drooping parchmented flesh slogged on to chain gang chants of "lotion, lotion"—the men that is. The women partied like it was 1969. Until they realized that their splashy merry making had a consequence with dark glop blotting their custom laundered attire.

"I'll never get this swamp stain out!" scowled Judy. Suzi concurred, "It's hell on natural fibers!"

Sy's bar on his phone was just enough for the utilities calculator to add up pooled resources of the group to file a lawsuit against the cruise line.

Algato assured, "Don't worry, I've got just the thing for that. Follow."

Snaking down around an imbedded cantilever of volcanic rock they descended a fern covered fault line shaded by rain forest canopy.

"Wait!" Chauncey shot an arm up as high as the bursitis red line, "Do you hear it?"

Drip, drip, drip . . .

"Aw Chaunce," snorted Judy,

"did ya forget to take the post nasal antihistamine again?"

"No, wait for it. Listen . . ."

Tinkling.

"Have we had an accident?" asked Algato massaging his glutes. They all looked around to take an ass check to see who couldn't 'hold it.' The tally yielded no creeping crotch watermarks. Through their shudder of relief and Sy's clicking jaw there it was, a tinkling—rhythmic, sparkling.

Algato laughed, "This way." And so they braved with stressed ankles a path of up thrusting rock and root through the deepest glen. The tinkling grew to a current heard but unseen until the embracing foliage parted in a proscenium proclaiming a river dappled gold with sun. Which was odd as the water was completely covered by the tropical umbrella.

The waters eddied around smooth shoals caressing soft sand bars tempting an afternoon lounge. Algato plunged his paw into the flow, "This is it! Spa Espana!"

A TIMOROUS DIPPING of corns, callouses and bunions exploded into a full throated swimming hole fray with Sy executing a perfect 10 Brooklyn Cannonball. Chauncey uncorked the strong strokes as the Swedish relay star that he was, circa 1966.

The women cavorted like sharks in chum. They noticed the swamp stains were completely bleached out, their clothes were spotless! How much better could life get?

Algato beckoned the gang to an adjoining grove, "Next spa stop!" He lifted a blind of compacted vines revealing a sunken tunnel opening. "Follow." He disappeared down under.

One by one they tiptoed in, which was easier now that their foot maladies vamoosed. Still they were careful out of habit not to trip and hurt a hip. The tunnel wound them to a cavern. In the center of the chamber was a fountain, iridescent, shimmering, wafting of musk. The stream flowed floating up in slow motion high to the ceiling then curved back around to amble down, bubble for an instant and drain into a subterranean canal to the river.

Activating a lock of sliding levers, Algato opened a chest made of semi precious gems encased in the wall. The chest contained quartz crystal tureen goblets with flecks of gold. "One at a time, each of you take a cup, fill it with water from the rising fountain"—which was a trick calling for a nimble flick of the wrist—"and gather around me."

Chauncey hesitated. Lifting such a hulking goblet would take at least two hands with an assist from his notoriously fickle lower back. But when he made his move, the goblet was weightless.

They formed a circle. Algato, the spoke of the wheel, offered a toast! "To Life!"

"To Life!" They quaffed the elixir.

Chauncey raised his hand higher than it had gone in decades, "When do we do the evacuation drill?"

"HEY JUDE, DID you catch Sy's act at the Conquistador Mall? He was computing so fast the cell phone calculator couldn't keep up with him!" Chauncey chortled. "He said he was just trying to keep up with Suzi's running tab, his cell battery boiling hot hot hot!"

"I was rather busy filling my cart."

"Huh, what?"

"When I went to try on clothes at Isabella's Boutique I had toned up," she swelled. Yes, it hadn't escaped Chauncey's attention that she no longer looked wasted, now blooming rosy cheeks, wrinkle and botox free. "I had to get a whole new wardrobe or I wouldn't have had a thing to wear the rest of the cruise. The mall had a great selection from Madrid of designer sizes amber accessorized."

Chauncey too had experienced the wonder of cinching up his belt passed the last hole. His nails had attained a natural manicure. The miracle to top it off—he needed a hairbrush! Chauncey celebrated. "Let's take a spin around the deck and see how far we get!" They promenaded, Judy in form fitting tennis cottons, Chauncey in surfer jammies. A stiff frontal breeze raced by. It was Sy.

It took a minute to tell since he was sporting a head of curly black locks with just a hint of tonsure. Sy stopped on the dime, turned around, pounded his chest. "I'm keeping up with Hurricane Suzi, and me now with one good jaw, two good knees no less and a 34-inch waist. No itch, no scratch. Musta done something right! See you later at the hop."

Chauncey and Judy approached the steel door barring the way determined, aquiline jaws set. But there was no need for muscle, as there often isn't when you have it. The door gave away to their tap, the door's sign abbreviated to "Cheers!" They stepped through the hatch, to starboard.

Greeted by their host for the evening, buff boy Tony, they entered a bevy of enticements. Ahhhh the Valhalla! Here was a smorgasbord of cheeses, chops, cream sauced turf 'n surf, continental concoctions of prawns swimming in twisted egg yolk pasta, capered oiled salads topped with kettle fried potato chips, all courses concluding with sentinels of sweets like multi-pudding layered coconut cake a la mode slathered with heaping dollops of rich butter frosting—a cornucopia of cholesterol, all you can eat at no cost to youthful arteries.

"Do you need antacid Chauncey? I saved a couple of cherry tablets your favorite?"

"Thanks dear, I'm groovy, no!"

"No?"

"No reflux, no pangs, no shits!"

"No bloat on this float!" Tony chimed. "See you at the lounge. By the way, you smell better."

CHAUNCEY COULDN'T BELIEVE it. He could swing Judy out wide after propelling the two of them in three moves across the dance floor of the Tenth Circle Lounge. No painful shoulder. No inhaler for congestion. No objecting joints begging for orthoscopic surgery. And Judy? Well, she was now a Rubenesque hourglass swaying on turbo charged knees. Meanwhile that whirling dervish from Brooklyn was center stage twirling Suzi perfectly poised.

They all were in top form, swinging to vintage hits spun by DJ Tony el Tigre. They pushed it well past the witching hour into the wee swilling gin and tonics to the limit.

Then, with dawn just below the horizon, The Rottendam turned sharply at an angle. The boat pitched this way and that, herky-jerky. Sy thought he was having a payback stroke.

"Not to worry," said Tony, "we're breaking in the new helmsman picked up at the last port. He was a pizza delivery guy."

The engines cut quick. As mics dropped over the dance floor, Tony took the lead mic. "And now hipsters, the fun starts! It's excursion time!"

"What," yelled Chauncey, "at the crack of dawn we go onshore?"

"No, my man, we don't need to go onshore."

"No?"

"No. We broadcast!"

"Broadcast?"

"A Boomer Blast!"

Chauncey noticed Judy, Suzi and Sy were transfixed, staring at the back of the bar. Between two mirrors hung an old conquistador painting of a bod in shining armor cradling mini metal flasks. There was something very familiar about the broad shoulders, chiseled breastplate, and those teeth!

Tony noticed. "That's Ponce de Leon's tracker. A shapeshifter."

"Whatta shape!" Judy and Suzi cougar cooed.

"Yo, he's quite the cat! He's a hit when he shows up to judge at Jaguar All British Field Meets. And of course he's the conductor for The Excursion."

Chauncey breathed deep. "The excursion to . . ."

"To the Fountain."

"Eureka!" Chauncey leapt without fear of injury. "The Fountain!"

"Yo, The Fountain."

"Of Youth!"

"Of Death."

"Death?" Chauncey found his hoarse again.

"Algato's Hideaway—you got a new lease on death. You never made it out of the underpass at the port alive."

"We wiped out over pizza?" Chauncey and Judy wailed.

"Well, you got an Afterlife—for the Dead."

Along with storm victims Sy and Suzie they chanted, "Afterlife. For. The. Dead."

"A perpetual cruise. It's all about the past today. Forever."

"Back to long term investing for maximum growth!" Sy phoned in the order.

"And no evacuation drills!" Chauncey chuffed, thoroughly relieved.

"Now let's have that fun." Tony shined. "Rev up your vocal chords—*Me Me Me Meee*. Follow the bouncing buoy on the monitors. Give the living hell. No dead air time now. Rock 'n' roll will never die! Cue 3–2–1 we're on!"

"*Madre de Dios*, the Ghost!" In his vendor hut, Louie de Paz scrambled for the ear corks to no avail. They were in the gullets of the mellowing lizards glowing tie-dye. And then the wave hit.

"PONYTAIL BURGER BABY TWISTAROO / REVS UP DADDY'S COUPE DO WANG GOO"

Moaning from the huts shook the palms. The islander appreciation did not go unrecognized.

"ROGER THAT—UNTIL NEXT TIME, THIS IS THE GHOST CRUISE—
THE FLYING HITSMAN!"

Robert Snashall is a DC outsider used to straddling the fault line. When not wrapped in Rose City weeklies, you'll most likely find him at Vista and Spring inhaling a Caesar.

Broadswords & Blasters No. 9

Review by Richard Krauss

"As always, we cannot express our gratitude enough to the people who submit to us, the people we publish, and the people who read us. We appreciate every shout out, and yes, we do read the reviews. Thanks for helping us make the literaray landscape just a touch weirder."

"From the Editors" by Matthew X. Gomez and Cameron Mount *B&B* No. 9

In "From the Editors," Matthew X. Gomez and Cameron Mount celebrate entering their third year of *Broadswords and Blasters*, and tip their hats to the other indie fiction mags publishing pulp-inspired short stories with a modern tang.

Luke Spooner's artwork has graced the covers of all nine *B&Bs* to date, but this issue's illustration is my favorite.

The title: *Broadswords and Blasters* evokes stories of swords crossing sorcery and spacemen zapping aliens. But its byline, "The pulp magazine with modern sensibilities," serves to broaden its scope further. This issue's stories embrace fantasy, supernatural, science fiction, crime, adventure, and horror.

Griffon Eggs by R.A. Goli

Kestrel and Zephariah face a harsh landscape as they climb a mountain in pursuit of a prized griffon egg. The lessons they learn along the way add to their burdens and conflate their futures. It's a story about choices, bad choices, the ones you either deny or regret.

Camera Obscura by Rex Weiner

An aggressive real estate developer seeks out buildings with an undesirable history. Suicides, spooks; whatever helps make them a bargain. After he guts them, they're reborn with swank and swagger. But his obsession finds him overdrawn, and the history of his latest acquisition begins a makeover of its own.

The Pole-House
by Ethan Sabatella

Mercenaries for hire, Connor and Eachann, en route to Orkneyjar need a place to stay the night when they reach Nidfell. Unfortunately, they're broke. But a shepherd gives them a way to solve both problems at once, pointing to the north. "There's a bet in the village; if a

stranger can stay the night in that house, we'll give them some coin." Never mind a witch's scorn-pole outside the place, or that fact that anyone who's stayed there either dies or is never seen again.

The Corsair's Daughter
by Cara Fox

The past rushes back to the corsair's daughter as she finds herself battling the demima-ton, a half-man, half-machine, that long ago claimed the life of her mother. And this time he's brought a pack of shadow wolves.

"His eyes were still human. She did not want to, but she could not stop herself from remembering the first time she stared into their chasmic depths. It was half a lifetime ago, but the sheer, breathtaking terror she felt when she looked into the eyes that seemed to pierce her soul was as raw and powerful as it had been on that fateful day. If she let it, the memory could easily undo her here and now."

Termination Clause
by Scotch Rutherford

Russians, sex slavers, and gangsters mix it up in Rutherford's satisfying crime fiction yarn. Atmospheric: "Dark and vacuous, the place was nearly empty, and smelled like rust." Brutal: "Somewhere between a whimper and a hoarse whisper, Kuznetsoc hissed, 'Please! Pull it out!'" And dicey till the end:

"Now you're fucked, my friend."

Old Haunting Grounds
by Matt Spencer

Crackerface and Cassias encounter a horde of nasties in the remains of New Spiralla. "They're shaped like bats, except with pinkish, baby-soft skin, and spindly, bent, human-looking legs stretched out behind them on either side of their stubby tails." Worse yet, Cassias can't stop the voice of his dead lover grating inside his head as the bloody battle rages on until its final unexpected thrust.

Quarter Past Ordinary
by C.W. Blackwell

A nightmarish creature hitches a ride on the train bound from Yuma, Arizona to Indio, California, making a mess of its victims along the route. A mysterious gunslinger is also onboard, hired to put an end to the slaughter. The story unfolds in jagged bursts, as the train ticks off milestones on the way to its final destination.

Courtship of the Queen of Thieves
by Vince Carpini

Scalrag and Zaline trade jabs and gibes as they vie for plunder over a series of risky heists. Both are adamant competitors but acknowledge a certain unspoken attraction for the other's nefarious skills and allure.

Olympian Six by Adam S. Furman

A super soldier and his team test their mettle against terrorists known for expertise with explosives, who have kidnapped the Governor. After a brief orientation session, the action and thrills are non-stop.

Wrap-Up

Broadswords and Blasters is a terrific package of top-drawer indie fiction for readers who enjoy a mix of genres that emphasize adventure and action. Its stories reflect their heritage of pulp magazine fare, freshly attuned to modern sensibilities of technology, voice, and culture.

Broadswords and Blasters No. 9 Spring 2019
Editors: Matthew X. Gomez and Cameron Mount
Cover: Luke Spooner
6″ x 9″, 123 pages
POD $6.99, Kindle $2.99
<broadswordsandblasters.com>

Manhunt Vol. 2 No. 5 July 1954

Manhunt 1954 part two

Synopses by Peter Enfantino

"Murder is an alley that runs parallel to the road we all walk, and it isn't as remote from you as you're apt to think."

"State Line" by Sam S. Taylor *Manhunt Detective Story Monthly* Sep. 1954

Vol. 2 No. 5 July 1954
144 pages, 35 cents

Chinese Puzzle by Richard Marsten, illo: Tom O'Sullivan (5000 words) ★★

A young Chinese girl goes into convulsions while doing her job as a phone solicitor and dies in front of her co-workers. Detectives Parker and Katz know strychnine poisoning when they see it. With the staccato dialogue and detailed procedural descriptions, it must have been relatively easy for those paying attention back in 1954, to discern that Richard Marsten was a pseudonym for Ed McBain.

My Game, My Rules by Jack Ritchie (2000 words) ★★1/2

Johnny takes a job from three desperate men. Since Johnny is an assassin, someone's going to die, but the hit man's mind may not be entirely on the target, but rather the target's moll.

Association Test by Hunt Collins, illo: Bill Ashman (1000 words) ★

Silly short-short about a psychiatrist and the word association test he conducts with his disturbed patient.

Two Grand by Charles Beckman, Jr. (3500 words) ★½

Doug Wallace flees L.A. after landing big debts with the mob. He heads for the hills where his brother, Jim, and wife, Sadie, live. Doug soon finds there's quite a bit of sexual tension in the air. In an amusing conversation with his brother, Doug finds out why:

> *"The war was rough on a lot of guys," (Jim) mumbled. "I guess I got no call to bitch. But why couldn't I have gotten it some other way? I wouldn't have minded losing an arm or a leg, Doug. You can still be a man with an arm or leg missin'. But not with–"*
>
> *It gradually dawned on Doug what the hell his brother was talking about. His eyes opened wide. So—now he understood it.*
>
> *He remembered vaguely that Jim had gotten the Purple Heart for being shot in Korea. But now he knew where Jim had been shot.*

"Two Grand" reads like the outline for one of those countless "Hill Tramp" backwoods novels that permeated the stands in the late 1950s. It's rushed and ultimately unsatisfying.

The Judo Punch by V. E. Theissen, illo: Tom O'Sullivan (1000 words) ★

A bent cop's wife suspects a man is following her and asks her husband to instruct her in the deadly art of judo. Nonsensical climax asks the reader to fill in all the blanks.

Sanctuary by W. W. Hatfield, illo: Houlihan (1500 words) ★★

Joe Varden has killed a prison guard and fled into the swamps to hide out with his cousin Pete and Pete's wife, Ginny. After Joe falls for Ginny, he devises a plan so he can have freedom and the beauty as well. This and "Two Grand" make for two very similar and very similarly lackluster tales.

Return by Evan Hunter (5000 words) ★★★

Matt Cordell is giving blood so he can raise booze money when he runs into old friend Sailor Simmons, who tells Matt some news: Matt's ex-wife Trina is back in town. He would have found this news out sooner or later because soon after he returns to his homeless shelter, Trina shows up, begging Matt to take her back. After a three paragraph hesitation, Cordell takes her back only to find that there's something up the ex's sleeve.

A good, solid entry, the penultimate in the Matt Cordell series. The "Return" in the title could refer to the return of Trina, the return of Matt's self-respect (albeit briefly), or the return of his sobriety since, as we take leave of him, he's still dry. But there is one more story to tell . . . .

I Want a French Girl by James T. Farrell (4000 words) ★½

Lawrence has come from America to Paris because he wants a French girl. He finds them—fat ones, skinny ones, dull ones—but not the one he's looking for. He's convinced that French girls are better lovers, but he's finding it hard to get proof. But for one throwaway final paragraph, this has no business being in a "Detective Story Monthly." The "In This Issue" blurb on the back cover touts it as "the story of a man with a single ambition, and of the way he was forced to fulfill it."

The Innocent by Muriel Berns, illo: Houlihan (1000 words) ★

Richard Leaman is brought up before a judge for rape and assault, but Richard's mother refuses to believe her son is anything but an angel.

Confession by John M. Sitan (3000 words) ★★★★

John Egan is a murderer. Not just any murderer. He takes his business seriously, with lots of preparation. His only motivation is "to insure the inclusion of my name in man's history and memory." Brutal serial sniper story is innovative long before the film *Targets* covered such ground. Sitan holds back no punches, here describing our first look at Egan's handiwork:

> *John Egan adjusted the rifle's telescopic sight again. It was quite easy to pick out the circle of light from the single lamp over the theatrical announcement plaque. The spot was a good target point. It was ten minutes after eleven and no one was about on the apartment house roof. He had counted eight persons crossing the circle of light. They had all been men. The ninth person was a woman. The white shoes and dress under a dark coat indicated she was a nurse. There was a young couple walking behind her. A policeman turned the corner.*
>
> *When the nurse reached the circle of light her head flew apart.*

Or this bit where Sitan pulls us, whether we want to be pulled or not, down even farther into Egan's twisted world:

> *He sighted on the junction again when he saw a woman and a little girl coming along. The girl was about five years old and wore a pink frilly dress. She was skipping a little ahead of the woman when she reached the junction. At that moment John Egan squeezed the trigger of his rifle. He watched the convulsive sideways jerk as the bullet thudded home. At his distance it appeared as if the child had stumbled. John did not look back until he had broken the sniper rifle down and put it in the trumpet case. When he did look back the woman was on her knees and screaming.*

I must admit while I was reading that passage, I fully expected the action would be halted in some way or that he would take out the mother. I never expected Sitan to go the distance. Obviously, with snipers a part of our everyday world, "Confession" is even more relevant now than when it was written nearly sixty years ago. But, further, the story examines the popularity of murder and the celebrity of evil.

Find a Victim by John Ross MacDonald, illo: Tom O'Sullivan (20,500 words) ★★★

Fifth and final appearance of Lew Archer in *Manhunt*. This time, Lew's on his way to deliver a report on drug trafficking to legislation in Sacramento when he happens upon a bleeding man on the side of a deserted highway. The man dies soon after Archer delivers him to a hospital. Before long, the PI discovers that the town has quite a few skeletons in its familial closet. The plot feels second-hand (or even third-hand) but the writing

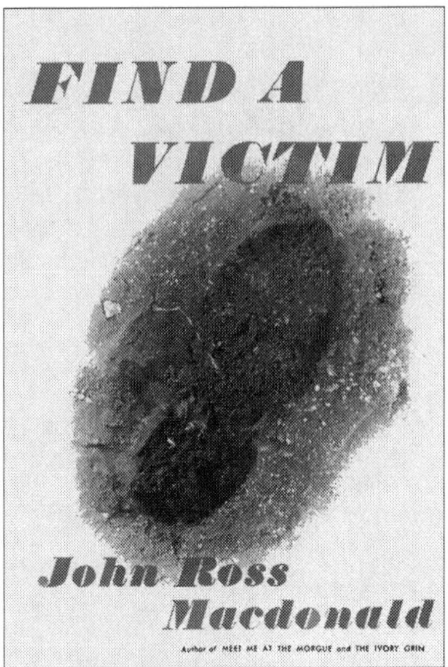

Find a Victim by John Ross Macdonald (Alfred A. Knopf, 1954)

crackles and keeps those pages turning, making even the obligatory conk on the head dazzling:

> *His fist came out from under the windbreaker, wearing something bright, and smashed at the side of my head.*
>
> *My legs forgot about me. I sat on the asphalt against the wall and looked at his armed right fist, a shining steel hub on which the night revolved. His face leaned over me, stark and glazed with hatred:*
>
> *"Bow down, God damn you . . . Bow down and kiss my feet"*

another passage, after Lew takes a nasty tumble:

> *It was a long fall straight down through the darkness of my head. I was a middle-aging space cadet lost between galaxies and out of gas. With infinite skill and cunning I put a grain of salt on the tail of a comet and rode it back to the solar system. My back and shoulder were burned raw from the sliding fall. But it was nice to be home.*

I still have problems with the cliched PI expository ("Suddenly I knew everything that had happened so I gathered everyone in one room and told them how it went down"), but this one has enough dazzle to make me overlook the trappings. That same year, Knopf released an expanded version of "Find a Victim" in novel form.

Helping Hand by Arnold Marmor (1000 words) ★★1/2

The DA can't get to mob boss Gomez unless O'Hara sings, but O'Hara says he'd rather fry in the electric chair than rat out Gomez. Nice twist elevates this above most short-shorts.

Vol. 2 No. 6 August 1954
144 pages, 35 cents

Identity Unknown
by Jonathan Craig,
illo: Houlihan (4500 words) ★★

The identity of a dead woman is traced through her fancy shoes. Very much like an 87th Precinct story.

Necktie Party by Robert Turner,
illo: Francis (2500 words) ★½

So a drunk walks into a bar and can't get served . . . A wildly gory horror story about a disgruntled customer with a straight razor and plenty of flesh around him. Not a bad set-up when done right. This isn't done right.

The Old Man's Statue
by R. Van Taylor, illo: Houlihan
(3000 words) ★½

What is the secret behind the

Manhunt Vol. 2 No. 6 August 1954

young man who, day in and day out, wipes the profane graffiti away from a statue in the town square? The new owner of the town paper is determined to get to the bottom of the mystery. *Peyton Place* pathos in a small Mississippi town with a climax right out of *Friday the 13th.* Two gory horror stories in one issue.

Effective Medicine

by B. Traven (4000 words) ★

An American doctor practicing in Mexico has a problem on

his hands. A local villager wants the doctor to find his adulterous wife or the doctor will feel the sharp edge of the man's machete.

Accident by John M. Sitan
(2000 words) ★★★

James Merrill has a strained relationship with his girlfriend, Gladys. They fight a lot. After one such argument, Gladys rushes out of the coffee shop they're both in and into traffic. Merrill spends the rest of the story making life hell for the unfortunate woman who ran down Gladys.

After hitting a home run last issue with "Confession," I doubted author Sitan could come up with another, but "Accident" is a solid thought-provoker with a wallop of a climax. It gets the job done, but I'd have liked to see it a bit longer. That may be because I enjoy the author's prose. This is the last of the three stories Sitan wrote for *Manhunt*. Other than a few stories in some of the harder men's magazines of the 1970s and 80s (*Gem*, *The Swinger*, and *BUF* [Big Up Front] *Swinger*), I can't find a trace of his writing. Any detectives out there?

I Don't Fool Around
by Charles Jackson (3000 words) ★★

George Burton is in love with the "new girl in town," Lynette McCaffrey, a lovely little tart who thinks nothing of revving up George's engine and then shutting it off at a moment's notice, with a smile. Much like "I Want a French Girl," this has no place in *Manhunt*. There's only a threat of violence hinted at in the final paragraph; nothing else makes this a crime story. I suspect it's simply because Jackson was a "name author" at the time (as author of *The Lost Weekend*) and John McCloud would have taken anything from him.

Frame by Frank Kane
(9000 words) ★★★

Johnny Liddell finds himself in a bit of a pickle once again. This time, an aging starlet his PI company has been bodyguarding has been found murdered, and all clues point to Liddell. Several thousands of dollars worth of diamonds and the jewels Johnny had been helping the woman to cash in, are MIA. The private dick has his work cut out for him as all his business associates in the case are looking out for No. 1 and denying any knowledge of the diamonds. Non-stop action, snappy dialogue, good hardboiled:

> *"This is for the kid, Murph." He slammed his fist against the big man's mouth. There was the sound of crunching teeth. The big man went staggering backward and fell across a table.*
>
> *"You won't be needing teeth where you're going."*

And Share Alike
by Charles Williams,
illo: Tom O'Sullivan
(21,000 words) ★★★★

Our narrator is hired by Diana James to steal a large amount of money from a woman named Madelon Butler. Mrs. Butler is married to a bank president, who has mysteriously disappeared after embezzling $120,000. Diana is convinced she can dig up the money before Madelon. First rule of noir: never trust a woman. Both females have so many double-crosses up their sleeves they need larger gowns. Williams ends it on a beautifully downbeat ending as the guy gets nothing but a jail cell. We find ourselves rooting for this guy even though the majority of his actions are immoral. He just happens to be a little less immoral than either of the female cast members.

Perhaps best known for the sea thriller *Dead Calm* (1963), Charles Williams was, according to Ed Gorman, "line for line, the best of all the Gold Medal writers . . . quiet and possessed of a melancholy that imbued each of his tales with a kind of glum decorum." Writer John D. MacDonald said that Williams was "one of the two or three best storytellers on the planet."

Here are a few lines from Williams himself, taken from "And Share Alike":

> *I stood there on the corner under a street light just holding the paper while the pieces fell all around me. It was too much. You could only get part of it at a time.*
>
> *And when I tried to tell them that I couldn't be suffering from any sense of guilt for killing Madelon Butler because I hadn't killed her, and not only that but if I had killed her I still wouldn't feel guilty about it because if I could only get my hands on her I'd gladly strangle her slowly to death right there before a whole courtroom full of people, including standing-room, and even pass out free refreshments if I had the money, it didn't help any.*

"And Share Alike" was expanded to novel form and released by Gold Medal later that year as *A Touch of Death*.

After his brief stint with *Manhunt* (3 short novels), Williams went

A Touch of Death by Charles Williams (Hard Case Crime-017, 2006) Cover by Chuck Pyle

on to write several more suspense novels (among them, *Man on the Run* [1958] and *Aground* [1960]). Like many of the classic Gold Medal crime novelists, the acclaim and notice didn't come until decades later when reprints and movie adaptations awakened a new generation to these "hidden treasures." Williams took his own life in 1975.

The film version of *Dead Calm*, skillfully directed by Philip (*Patriot Games*) Noyce is a nail-biting, claustrophobic thriller set almost entirely on a boat in the middle of the ocean that made Nicole Kidman a star.

Yard Bull by Frank Selig, illo: Houlihan (1000 words) ★★

Security guard for the railroad recounts his early days as a train-hopper.

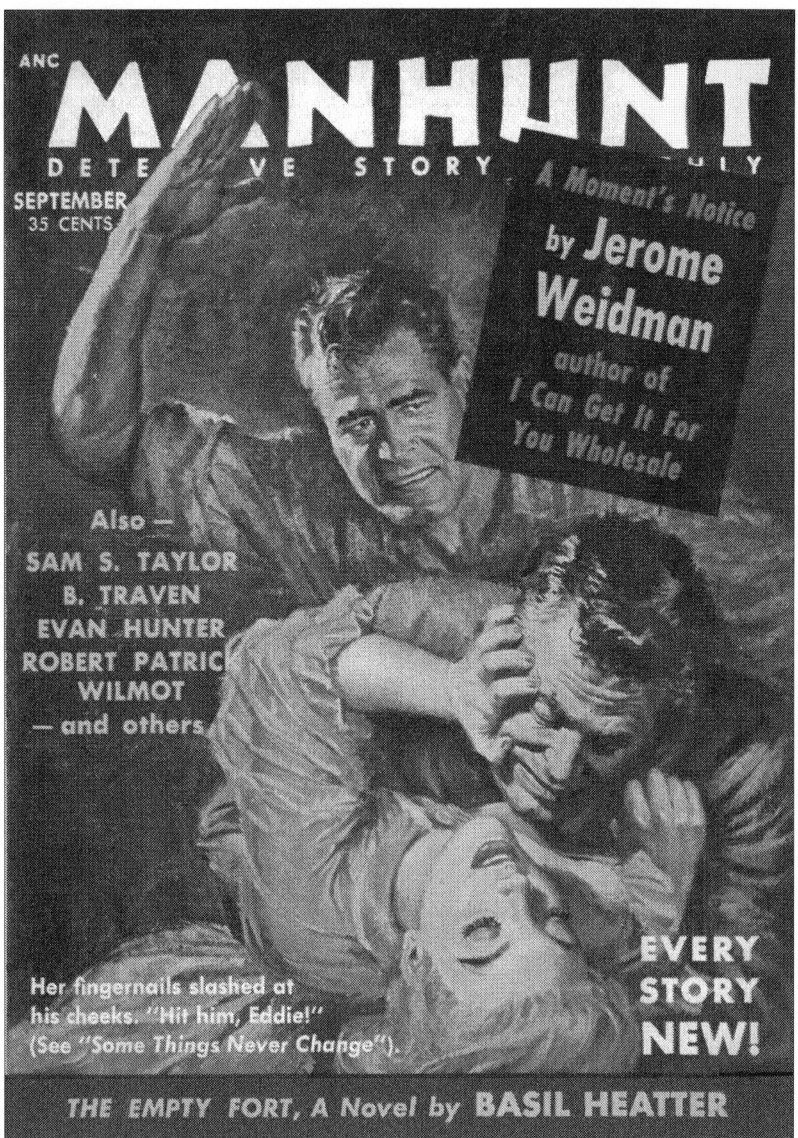

Manhunt Vol. 2 No. 7 September 1954

Vol. 2 No. 7 September 1954
144 pages, 35 cents

The Witness by John Sabin, illo: Houlihan (3000 words) ★★

Mark Hagan begins to question the merits of being a good Samaritan. He witnesses the murderous Earl Splade gun down a man in cold blood and reports it to the police. Now, it seems the police can't protect Mark from the murderer, who's back on the streets in no time. Abrupt but satisfying climax. This was Sabin's only appearance in *Manhunt* or any crime magazine for that matter.

Bedbug by Evan Hunter (1000 words) ★

A paranoid husband interrogates his mad wife. Or is it the other way around? When does a 1000-word short story feel like a 100,000-word novel? When it's filled with dreadful dialogue and a story that is going nowhere. This story and "Association Test" (from July's issue) prove that Evan Hunter needs a few more words to get his groove going.

State Line by Sam S. Taylor, illo: Houlihan (6500 words) ★★★

Linoleum salesman rolls into Vegas and is immediately smitten with a rich beauty. Like most *Manhunt* dames, this one's got something up her sleeve. She's got an old hubby who's become a burden, and now she's searching for a way to become a rich widow. What seems to be heading down the path of a Fred MacMurray film veers down a dirt road to something completely different. This would have made a nice episode of *Alfred Hitchcock Presents* (it is slightly reminiscent of the classic "One More Mile to Go" from the second season of *AHP*).

Night Watch by Jonathan Craig, illo: Dick Francis (4500 words) ★★

Sergeants Sharber and Curran, Homicide, 9th Precinct, catch a strange case: the man's been shot in the head and when they dig further they find kiddie porn and heroin. Luckily for the detectives, the murderer falls right into their hands and confesses. This has the most abrupt ending I've ever come across. I literally searched the magazine for a "Continued from page 42" but my copy is lacking any such closure.

Tin Can by B. Traven, Illo: Tom O'Sullivan (4000 words) ★★★1/2

Natalio Salvatorres is looking for a wife and finds her in Filomena Gallardo, a young peasant whose father is only too happy to sell her for a new pair of pants and a few bottles of tequila. Moving to a mining town to find work, Natalio is happy in his new life until one day he finds his wife has run off with another man. Seeking revenge, Natalio crafts an explosive in a tin can and heads for the hut where his wife is attending a party. Unfortunately for Natalio, the only person killed in the blast is a friend of Filomena's:

> *The occupants of the hut saw the bomb and jumped out of the hut without even taking the time for a shout of horror. This took them less than half a second. At once a terrific explosion followed, sending the hut up a hundred feet in the air.*
>
> *Of the six people who had been inside, five escaped without so much as a scratch. The sixth, the young woman of the couple that owned the hut, was not so fortunate.*
>
> *This woman had, at the very moment the bomb made its appearance at the party, been busy making fresh coffee in the corner of the hut farthest from the door. She had neither seen the bomb nor noted the rapid and speechless departure of her guests. Consequently she accompanied the hut on its trip upward. And since she had been unable in so short a time to decide which part of the hut she would like best to travel with, she landed at twenty different places in the vicinity.*

The Rebellion of the Hanged by B. Traven (Alfred A. Knopf, 1952) Cover by Joseph Low

As you can tell from that passage, this is a dark comedy. "Tin Can" gets even wittier when Natalio faces trial for his crime.

B. Traven was the author of *Treasure of the Sierra Madre* (1927), *The Rebellion of the Hanged* (1936), and several other acclaimed novels. His life and identity were something of a mystery. According to his *Manhunt* bio, not even his agent knew his true identity.

Ambition by Patrick Madden (1500 words) ★★★

The cops have a cold-blooded killer dead to rights, but the murderer seems almost happy they do. For such a short story, this is an effective commentary on what someone will do to achieve that "15 minutes."

A Moment's Notice
by Jerome Weidman, illo: Houlihan (9000 words) ★★★★

Dr. Holcomb, eighty years old, realizes he hasn't much time left, but before he goes he must atone for a sin his son committed ten years earlier, an evil act Dr. Holcomb helped cover up for fear of scandal. When a similar situation rears its ugly head, and his son is again the villain, the doctor finds a way to make peace with himself. Or does he?

Though I have problems with the logic the doctor shows in solving his problem at the climax, this is a riveting story. Too often, I've found when a big name drops into the *Manhunt* headquarters, they seldom deliver. Here's a case of the big name delivering and then some. A passage, referring to Holcomb's son, Robert, might well have been prescient of today's celebrities and their various foibles:

> *How did one deal with the wicked who were ignorant of the meaning of wickedness, with the sinner who had no conception of sin?*
>
> *The only occasion on which Robert seemed to be aware that he had done anything the world condemned came at the moments when he was caught.*

Jerome Weidman (1913–1998) is best known for his Great Depression novel, *I Can Get It for You Wholesale* (1937) and for co-writing the Joan Crawford vehicle, *The Damned Don't Cry* (1950).

Every Morning by Richard Marsten, illo: Houlihan (1500 words) ★★

A governess plays cruel games with her hired help every morning until he can take it no more and violence ensues.

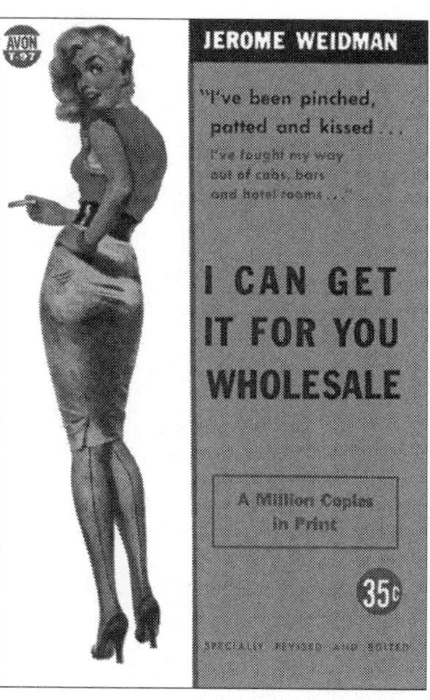

I Can Get It for You Wholesale by Jerome Weidman (Avon T-97, 1955)

Some Things Never Change
by Robert Patrick Wilmot,
illo: Tom O'Sullivan (2500 words) ★

Kerrigan flies back to England to reclaim the love he lost during the Second World War. She's got other plans for the sap. But is he a sap? A first: 500 words of set-up, 2000 words of expository. Outrageous and clunky expository to boot!

The Empty Fort by Basil Heatter,
illo: Houlihan (14,500 words) ★★★

Flake, captain of the Jezebel, is hired by Mangio to haul in tons of shrimp. Flake is the best at his business; he knows it, and demands a larger cut from Mangio. Not one to take insubordination, Mangio hires shipmate Cutter to kill Flake and make it look like an accident. Cutter knocks Flake overboard during a nasty storm, but the captain is from the "die hard" school and survives long enough to be rescued by a passing boat. Exciting sea adventure, reminiscent of Charles Williams' novels, with a violent finale at the titular structure.

The son of radio broadcaster Gabriel Heatter, Basil Heatter was the author of several novels including *The Dim View* (Signet, 1948), *Sailor's Luck* (Lion, 1953), *The Mutilators* (Gold Medal, 1962), *Virgin Cay* (Gold Medal, 1963), *Harry and the Bikini Bandits* (Gold Medal, 1971) and two adventures of Tim Devlin, marine insurance man, *The Golden Stag* and *Devlin's Triangle* (both Pinnacle, 1976). Mugged and Printed mentions an upcoming Lion novel called *Powder Snow*. This was retitled *Act of Violence* for publication in 1954. Heatter's novels accentuated the adventure whether it be icy mountain tops (*Act of Violence*), wrecked ships (*Virgin Cay*), or gun smuggling in Europe (*The Mutilators*).

The Promise by Richard Welles
(1000 words) ★

Nothing more than the outline for a short story about a cop who goes after his brother, who is wanted for murder.

Vol. 2 No. 8 October 1954
144 pages, 35 cents

The Beatings by Evan Hunter, illo:
Ray Houlihan (3500 words) ★★★★

"Men can become good neighbors when their common mortar is despair." Another visit to the hell populated by Ex-PI, current drunk Matt Cordell. This time, Matt's helping out his fellow winos, who find themselves under attack by a pack of violence-hungry teenagers. Interestingly enough, "The Beatings"

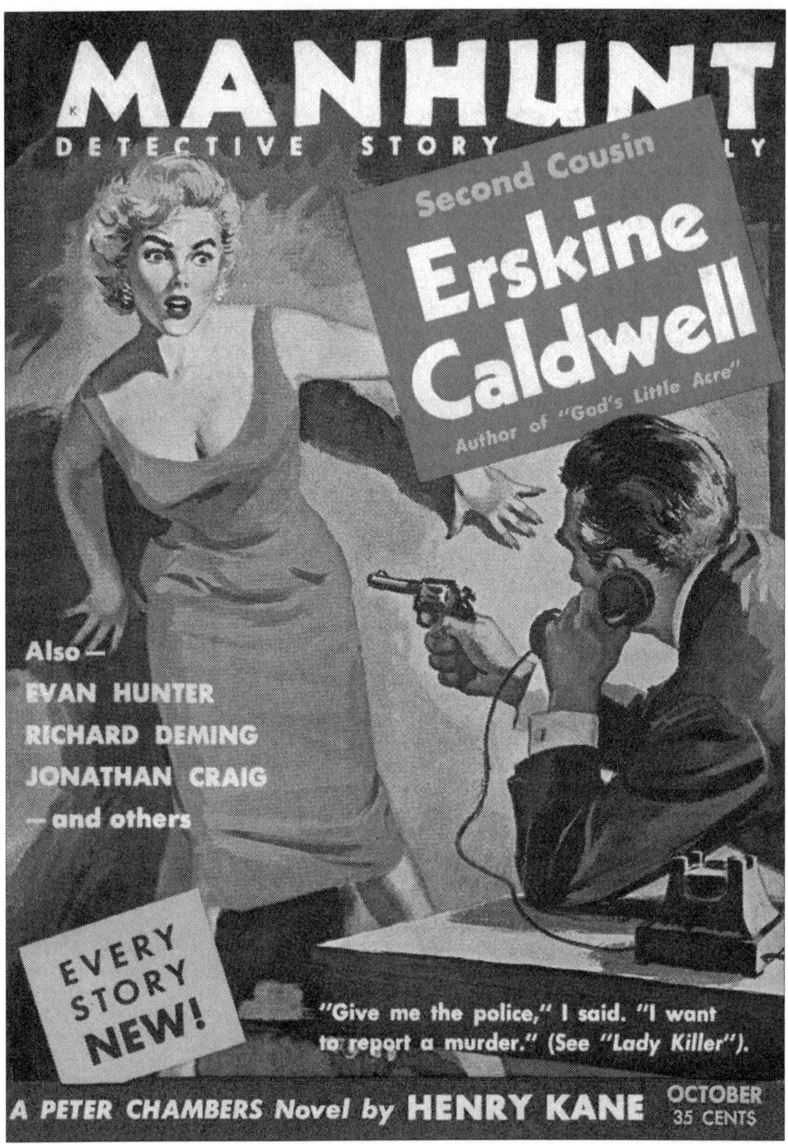

Manhunt Vol. 2 No. 8 October 1954

starts off with one of Ed McBain's patented soliloquies of the city: "the city wore August like a soiled flannel shirt." Eighth and final Matt Cordell story is also the best of the bunch.

The Bargain by Charles Beckman, Jr., illo: Tom O'Sullivan (3000 words) ★★★

Frank and his wife Mavis are vacationing at their mountain cabin when a murderer, hiding from the police, takes them hostage. To win their freedom, Mavis must give the man what he wants. Nice twist when we find that Mavis might have other reasons for going along with this killer's demands.

Clean Getaway by William Vance (5500 words) ★★★

Police chief Mark Nadine closes in on a couple of murderers at a roadside inn. The pair make a getaway but not before Mark makes a startling discovery: the woman of the pair is his wife, long gone but not forgotten. A well-written noir, very much cut from the cloth of Jim Thompson, but a few too many questions left unanswered for my tastes. Second and final *Manhunt* story for Vance (although this story would be retitled "Lust or Honor" for the December 1966 issue). William Vance wrote westerns, under his name as well as the pseudonym George Cassidy, for such pulps as *Star Western*, *2-Gun Western*, *Dime Western*, and *Best Western*, as well as crime stories for *Trapped*, *Terror Detective*, and *Mike Shayne*.

Terror Detective Story Magazine No. 2 Dec. 1956 with William Vance's "Murderer's Manual"

Laura and the Deep, Deep Woods by W. B. Hartley, illo: Tom O'Sullivan (2000 words) ★★

Teenaged Eddie gets his first glimpse of "what sex really is" when he happens upon cute little Laura in the deep, deep woods. By no stretch of the imagination, a *Manhunt* story. Reads more like an excerpt from a Twain novel. This was the only story Hartley wrote for *Manhunt*.

Second Cousin by Erskine Caldwell, illo: Tom O'Sullivan (2000 words) ★1/2

Pete Ellrod comes home to find his wife's second cousin, once removed, has moved into his house, and the wife is being a bit stubborn about the situation. Pete doesn't want the cousin around, as second cousins, once removed, historically have a tendency to want favors granted. Second story by Erskine Caldwell to see print in *Manhunt* (with three to follow) has the same problem I had with its predecessor: it doesn't belong in a "Detective Story Monthly." It would be better served in *The Saturday Evening Post* or one of the other slicks of the 1950s.

Love Affair by Richard Deming, illo: Ray Houlihan (2000 words) ★

This homophobic tale of two cops and the "woman" they pick up in a sleazy bar is about as subtle as the bar's name: The Purple Dragon. You can see the "twist" coming at you two pages in. Deming is so much better than this would lead one to believe.

Lady Killer by Richard Marsten, illo: Francis (2500 words) ★★

Charlie Rawlings is the best hit-man money can buy. Now George

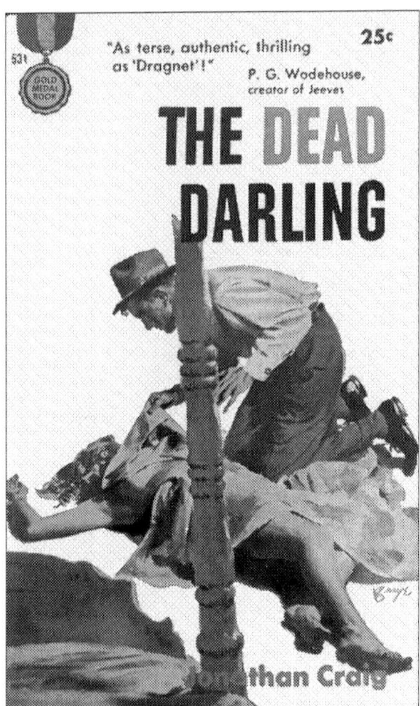

The Dead Darling by Jonathan Craig (Gold Medal 531, 1955) Cover by Baryé

Manelli, mob boss, needs Rawlings to silence an old moll of George's. She's about to sing to the cops about his organization, and she knows enough to bring his comfy world crashing around him. No relation to the 87th Precinct novel McBain (Marsten) would write in 1958.

The Dead Darling
by Jonathan Craig, illo: James Sentz
(5000 words) ★★1/2

Detectives Rayder and Selby are called in to investigate what appears at first to be a suicide (a girl with her head in the oven), but it quickly becomes apparent that what they're actually dealing with is a murder. This girl spent a lot of her free time bedding married men.

Though Ed McBain's 87th Precinct novels became world famous and sold in the millions, Jonathan Craig's Pete Selby[1] and Stan Rayder stories (aka The 18th Precinct) actually pre-dated the 87th by two years. "The Dead Darling" was expanded into the first Pete Selby novel of the same name in 1955. Craig wrote three 18th Precinct stories for *Manhunt* before turning his attention to the novels. The series morphed in a way into a second set of procedurals Craig wrote for *Manhunt* (the Police Files) but more on that in a future installment.

That Stranger, My Son
by C. B. Gilford, illo: Ray Houlihan
(3000 words) ★

Paul and his father are grieving the drowning death of Paul's

[1] There were ten Pete Selby novels in all:
- ☐ *The Dead Darling* (1955)
- ☐ *Morgue for Venus* (1956)
- ☐ *The Case of the Cold Coquette* (1957)
- ☐ *The Case of the Beautiful Body* (1957)
- ☐ *The Case of the Petticoat Murder* (1958)
- ☐ *The Case of the Nervous Nude* (1959)
- ☐ *The Case of the Village Tramp* (1959)
- ☐ *The Case of the Laughing Virgin* (1960)
- ☐ *The Case of the Silent Stranger* (1964)
- ☐ *The Case of the Brazen Beauty* (1966)

The original Gold Medal paperbacks had typically gorgeous covers by George Mayers, George Gross, and Stanley Zuckerberg. When Belmont/Tower reprinted the series in 1973, the publishers opted to grace the covers (with one exception—*The Dead Darling*—a sharp painting that could have come from the Gold Medal art gallery) with generic, ugly men's adventure leftovers. The casual newsstand browser would not have been able to tell the difference between Selby and The Sharpshooter or The Marksman, two very bad 1970s Belmont adventure series. Belmont also chose to number both *Morgue for Venus* and *Laughing Virgin* as No. 6 in the series, ostensibly to confuse the reader or because they just didn't care enough to check the number of the previous book.

brother. The boy's father is convinced that Paul could have saved his brother's life. There's something to those suspicions, of course. The first appearance by prolific short story writer C. B. Gilford in *Manhunt* (he would contribute a total of 12 stories throughout the run). Gilford became a staple of *Alfred Hitchcock's Mystery Magazine* (seeing 80 stories published between the July 1957 issue and his last appearance in October 1980) as well as most of the other crime digests of the 1950s and 1960s. Five of his stories were dramatized on *Alfred Hitchcock Presents/Hour.*

One of a Kind by Ben Smith, illo: Ray Houlihan (1000 words) ★

Sordid short-short about rape and the degrees of evil.

The Famous Actress by Harry Roskelenko, illo: Lee(1500 words) ★

Wandering the streets of Paris, a man picks up a woman he later finds is a well-known actress, researching a role. Unfortunately for the lady, the man is a bit of an "actor" himself.

Candlestick by Henry Kane, illo: James Sentz (16,500 words) ★★

Peter Chambers is enlisted by police lieutenant Louis Parker to help solve the murder of publicity mega-agent Max Keith. The agent has been clobbered with a gold candlestick, and the lieutenant is up to his neck in suspects. One of the suspects is the victim's sister, who stands to inherit a big chunk of the family inheritance once her brother is dead. Chambers knows the girl is innocent (well, innocent in *Manhunt* is a relative term) since, in a laugh-out-loud coincidence, he was bedding her when he got the call! Not really as grating as the other Chambers novellas but still about double the length it needs to be.

Peter Enfantino writes about various horror and war comic books on <barebonesez.blogspot.com> twice weekly, covering the Warren Publishing books, Atlas /Marvel pre-code horror books, and DC's war comics.

Internet

Poem by Clark Dissmeyer

Reading science fiction just forty years ago in Kansas,
one might have an adventure, some fun with imagination.

Now its tentacles reach from the dull horizon
into our homes, bodies, through our fingers into our minds,
create nightmares as endless as the plains.

COMING JULY 2019

Opening Lines

Selections from digests featured in this edition.

"Joe Varden stood in swamp water up to his armpits, and his feet kept sinking deeper into the ooze."
"Sanctuary" by W.W. Hatfield
Manhunt Detective Story Monthly July 1954

"Elsewhere I have set down, for whatever interest they have in this, the 25th Century, my personal recollections of the 20th Century."
"Armageddon–2419 A.D." by Philip Francis Nolan *Amazing Stories* April 1961

"In the last analysis, you have to have luck, Abner Vincent was thinking as he parked the station wagon and put a dime into the parking meter with the careless abandon of a man about to undergo an amputation."
"And Then No More . . ." by Jay Tyler
Startling Mystery Stories No. 8 Spring 1968

"Chapil raised the silenced automatic, held it firmly with both hands, sighted carefully, felt the subtle shifting in his heart, hesitated, and the hazy form ahead of him had turned the corner."
"Figure in Flight" by John Lutz
Charlie Chan No. 2 February 1974

"I suspect the last time someone was stabbed to death with a letter opener was 1950."
"Private Justice" by Steven Gore
Alfred Hitchcock May/June 2019

"Shayne looked up to see the third man standing in the doorway, the highpowered rifle in his hands lined up squarely on the detective's forehead."
"Payoff In Blood" by James Reasoner writing as Brett Halliday *Mike Shayne* March 1980

"From the instant he stepped inside the ancient house, a *casa antiqua* as the realty ad said, gazing around at its blood-colored adobe walls, Wilson felt something stirring deep within his gut, something about the way the sun streamed through cracks in the massive wooden front door catching dust swirls in its light."
"Camera Obscura" by Rex Weiner
Broadswords and Blasters No. 9 Spring 2019

"The captain said, 'You've been drinking,' and that was all he said about it so Smith thought he couldn't be looking so badly; yet Smith knew it wasn't the whisky—or anyway, not just the whisky—that made him look as if he had been hit in the face with a ton of wet towels."
"Good-By Hannah" by Steve Fisher
All Mystery Oct–Dec 1950

"The weight of the gun could not have been more than a pound, but to Amy Tobin it seemed to drag her arm down like a cannonball."
"Death on the Strip" by Gary Brandner
Mike Shayne Mystery Magazine Dec. 1979

"Full of forebodings and the most unique tensions that an adult Chem had ever experienced, Kelexel the Investigator came down into the storyship where it hid beneath the ocean."
"The Heaven Makers" (part one) by Frank Herbert *Amazing Stories* April 1967

"One afternoon, on coming home from the cotton field where I had worked all day long, I noted, outside the barbed wire

fence of the bungalow I was living in, a Mexican peasant squatting on the bare ground."
"Effective Medicine" by B. Traven
Manhunt Detective Story Monthly Aug. 1954

"When King Edward VI of England died in the year 1553, his sister and successor Mary (who has gone down in history as 'Bloody Mary') promptly sent for the dead King's favorite astrologer. She asked him to predict her future."
"The Man Who Had Supernatural Powers" by John Charr *Science Fiction Digest* No. 2 1954

"The blood-red Mercury with the twin-mounted 7.6 mm Spandaus cut George off as he was shifting lanes."
"Dogfight on 101" by Harlan Ellison
Amazing Stories Sep. 1969

"A thin fog hung over the high iron gates of the isolated estate on Half Moon Bay south of San Francisco."
"The Temple of the Golden Horde" by Dennis Lynds writing as Robert Hart Davis
Charlie Chan No. 3 May 1974

"My shoulders ached from three hours of driving to start with, and I don't like being grabbed."
"Dead In Friday" by James Reasoner
Spiderweb No. 3 Summer 1982

"'Man, I don't get how you can stand this place!' Crackerface shifts in the big, ornately carved chair that's practically a throne, peering at the vast, cobweb-strewn ruins of the great drink hall, in the royal temple of what used to be New Spiralla."
"Old Haunting Grounds" by Matt Spencer
Broadswords and Blasters No. 9 Spring 2019

"August was a shimmering canopy of heat, August was the open mouth of a blast furnace, August was a hot cliché, all the hot clichés, and the city wore August like a soiled flannel shirt."
"The Beatings" by Evan Hunter
Manhunt Detective Story Monthly Oct. 1954

"In spite of the laws of gravity, the moon's attraction for a small boy is far greater, I maintain, than for any other object in our solar system."
"Will Your Child Visit the Moon" by Jack Cluett *Science Fiction Digest* No. 1 1954

Advertiser's Index

Index to The Digest Enthusiast No. 1–10

Interviews **Issue** **Pg**

Profiles/Artist's Statements **Issue** **Pg**

Reviews* **Issue** **Pg**

*Reviews written by Peter Enfantino, Ron Fortier, Richard Krauss, Joe Wehrle, Jr. and D. Blake Werts.

Verse **Issue** **Pg**

55179409R00094

Made in the USA
Middletown, DE
15 July 2019